The Time of the Crime

The Time of the Crime

Phenomenology, Psychoanalysis, Italian Film

Domietta Torlasco

Stanford University Press

Stanford, California

Stanford University Press
Stanford, California

Printed in the United States of America on acid-free, archival-quality paper

Library of Congress Cataloging-in-Publication Data

Torlasco, Domietta, 1968-
  The time of the crime : phenomenology, psychoanalysis, Italian film /
Domietta Torlasco.
    p. cm.
  Includes bibliographical references and index.
  ISBN 978-0-8047-5802-4 (cloth : alk. paper)
  1. Detective and mystery films--Italy--History and criticism. 2. Time in
motion pictures. I. Title.
  PN1995.9.D4T67 2008
  791.43'6556--dc22   2008006699

Designed by Bruce Lundquist
Typeset at Stanford University Press in 11/13.5 Adobe Garamond

Contents

Acknowledgments

I WROTE THIS BOOK DURING MY APPOINTMENT as a Harper-Schmidt Fellow and a Collegiate Assistant Professor in the Humanities at the University of Chicago but developed its blueprint while at the University of California, Berkeley. My gratitude goes to Kaja Silverman, Judith Butler, Barbara Spackman, and Anton Kaes, who inspired and supported my work as a doctoral student in the Department of Rhetoric. Kaja Silverman provided invaluable guidance on my dissertation as well as precious institutional assistance. The rigorous and adventurous close readings that distinguish her seminars were for me a decisive experience. I especially wish to thank Judith Butler, who first spoke to me of a book and offered, together with the most lucid insights, constant encouragement and advice. My gratitude also goes to the friends and colleagues who read different parts of this work and responded with remarkably smart and helpful comments—Homay King, Greg Forter, Lynne Layton, Sharon Willis, Patricia White, and Vivian Sobchack. I also wish to thank Norris Pope and Emily-Jane Cohen, for their interest in the project and professionalism; the Stanford University Press readers, for their generous and thought-provoking insights; Mariana Raykov, who patiently guided me through the last steps of the publication process; and Andrew Frisardi, who edited the manuscript with such a careful hand. I am deeply grateful to Scott Combs, for our interminable discussions on cinema and death; to Theresa Schwartzman, who brilliantly edited the last chapter; to Nasrin Qader and Susan Gayle Levine, for their friendship and counsel during the last phases of the composition process; to Frida Ravasi, my first mentor; and to A. B. Scott. Special thanks to my family, particularly to my sister Diletta.

A shorter version of Chapter 1 appeared in *Camera Obscura* 22, no. 1 64 (2007): 77–111; and a shorter version of Chapter 2 appeared in *Psychoanalysis, Culture, and Society* 10 (August 2005): 138–50, and in *Desire of the Analysts: Psychoanalysis and Cultural Criticism*, ed. Paul A. Miller and Greg Forter (Albany: State University of New York Press, 2008). I thank the editors for permission to reprint.

The Time of the Crime

Introduction

WHETHER IT ALL BEGAN WITH FILM OR CRIME, it is impossible for me to say. I grew up in the shadow of Luchino Visconti's *Ossessione* (*Obsession*, 1943), the first neorealist film and also the free adaptation of James M. Cain's *The Postman Always Rings Twice* (1934), and by the age of fifteen I was responding to the frustration of not having a VCR by recording sounds and voices from Michelangelo Antonioni's *L'avventura* (*The Adventure*, 1960). For years I kept a photograph of Anna, the woman who vanishes at the outset of the film and whose disappearance is gradually forgotten, between the pages of my date book. Probably a still from the set, the picture shows Anna, dark hair and dark eyes, dressed in white, leaning against an iron gate. Her look is oblique, directed toward an indeterminate zone beyond the frame, defying a spectator whom she addresses through avoidance—an impossible look, the promise or threat of a double disappearance. Film critic Pascal Bonitzer brilliantly writes of this "disappearance of disappearance," the mark of a crisis that will gradually dismantle the detective story, undermining its certainties and opening it to ontological interrogation. As if the puzzle in pieces, and not the process of its reassemblage, exercised the strongest attraction, several of Antonioni's films seem to adopt the model of the police investigation only to undo it. What is left is a world of fragmentation and dispersion, which the characters traverse as "detectives without purpose and out of place," caught in a web that disconnects them. "Un giallo alla rovescia," is the director's own definition of *The Adventure*, a detective story "back to front," turned upon itself, reversed.[1]

The radicalness of Antonioni's challenge comes into sharper focus as one turns to Ernst Bloch's essay "A Philosophical View of the Detective Novel." On the trail of the uncanny as it has appeared in literature and drama from Sophocles to Edgar Allan Poe, Bloch writes of the detective story as a genre devoted to the "search for that remoter 'something,' which is already close at hand,"[2] analyzing its incessant "knitting and knotting" and identifying its fundamental characteristics—the suspense connected with the process of guessing; the conjectural activity that, through a careful evaluation of apparently insignificant details, leads to the act of discovery; and, most notably, the omission of the pivotal event: the detective story opens on a crime that has already been committed. It is this very omission, Bloch emphasizes, that provides the genre with its specific narrative form, namely, "the form of a picture puzzle."[3] Whether relying on induction, like Sherlock Holmes, or on intuition, like Hercules Poirot, the detective looks at the crime scene from a "micrological" perspective, seeking out those unintentional and overlooked signs that will allow him to shed light into an original, prenarrative darkness, that is, to transform the unnarrated event into a narrative sequence. What happens to this form when *The Adventure* unfolds as a story of forgetfulness and decreasing tension—of an investigation that forgets itself, leaving behind a crime which might or might not have taken place—is thus something other than a plot variation. And it can be said to produce an effect well outside the boundaries of the genre proper if, like Bloch, one recognizes that the same process of discovery and reconstruction also characterizes the works of writers such as Ibsen and Freud, structuring the very relation between light and darkness, revelation and disguise, surface and depth around which they revolve.

My fascination with the crisis of the detective genre expresses more than a subjective preference for certain formal and narrative strategies. Numerous critics, from Walter Benjamin and Siegfried Kracauer to contemporary film scholars like Tom Gunning, have identified the detective story as the genre in which modernity and its visual regimes are both exposed and defamiliarized. The increasing abstraction of space and time, the expansion of perceptual experience through technologies as diverse as the railway and the cinematograph, the standardization of techniques for the identification and control of the individual in the crowd of the big city—all these aspects of modern life find expression in a textual universe structured around the figures of the detective and the criminal. If the detective wants to know the truth of the crime, he needs to interpret the traces of what is no longer there, reading clues and symptoms with a passion for conjectural reasoning that, according to Carlo Ginzburg, aligns him with the psychoanalyst and the historian alike. "Reality is opaque," writes Ginzburg in his famous article on Morelli, Freud, and Holmes, "but there are certain points—clues, symptoms—which allow us to decipher it."[4] The fact that the photograph, with its strong indexical and iconic ties to the referent, constitutes the ultimate tool in the process of detection speaks to the visual nature of the investigator's challenge: the determination to see again what had once occurred, to seize the image of a time now passed. Such a desire to see is so strong that, Gunning reminds us, "the camera recording the very fact of malefaction appears in drama, literature, and early film before it was really an important process of criminal detection."[5] Catching the criminal in the act, then, expresses the desire not only to attach guilt to an identifiable body, but also to "see through" the obscurity of the crime, reconnecting the present of the trace to the past of the deed.[6] Seeing is at once this movement of translation from opacity to clarity and the guarantee of a reordering of time. "Detective fiction," we read in a study on the art and ideology of suspense, "is preoccupied with the closing of the logico-temporal gap that separates the present of the discovery of crime from the past that prepared it. It is a genre committed to the act of recovery, moving forward in order to move back."[7] What happens, then, when the investigative paradigm deteriorates as it does in *The Adventure*? What happens not only to our desire to see into the past but also to the very possibility of isolating the past from the present and the future, locating the detective and ourselves, the spectators, in a time that is successive to the time of the crime?

The work I am presenting is dedicated to the study of the relationship between time and vision as it emerges in five Italian films, all following the experience of *The Adventure*: Antonioni's *Blow-up* (1966) and *Professione: Reporter* (*The Passenger*, 1975), Liliana Cavani's *Il portiere di notte* (*The Night Porter*, 1973), Pier Paolo Pasolini's *Edipo Re* (*Oedipus Rex*, 1967), and Bernardo Bertolucci's *La strategia del ragno* (*The Spider's Stratagem*, 1970). The center around which these films revolve is the image of the crime scene—the spatial and temporal configuration in which a crime is committed, witnessed, and investigated. Uniquely influenced by both neorealism and the tradition of film noir, these films present us with a crime to be "seen," not once and for all but over and over again, in the folds of the landscape as well as on the faces of people and things. They appear as strange and unsolvable detective stories in which continuous, linear time dissolves, and the privileges of the seeing eye are challenged by the very scene under analysis. In fact, it is by dilating or contracting the detective story to its extreme limits that these films articulate forms of time which defy any clear-cut distinction between past, present, and future, offering us a temporality which cannot be calculated, determined with certainty, but only made visible. "*In detective fiction*," claims Joan Copjec in her work on film noir, "*to be is not to be perceived, it is to be recorded*"—here, perception overturns the power of counting, of "making up people," becoming the very texture through which the subject is dispersed, blurred almost to the point of fading or disappearance, and time is released.[8]

Whether a photographer, a journalist, or a mythical solver of riddles, in these films, the investigator who looks back at the crime scene to discover the truth comes to occupy a position of passivity with respect to the object of his quest—he searches, and is found; he looks, and is seen. Yet, the picture of the past by which he is gradually confronted is anything but external to him. What appears in front of the investigator's eyes is not the past as it was, but the past as it will have been in relation to the time of his search. If the detective story proper begins with a murder that has already been committed, a death that has already taken place, the death which seems to count the most in these films is the one that is yet to occur—the investigator's own death. It is in the anticipation of this death, which the investigator is called to face not as a fact but as a possibility, as the assumption of his own finitude, that the search unfolds. Again and again, the crime scene draws the detective into a time that I can describe only by means of a compound tense, the future anterior.

For Jacques Lacan the time of our "being-for-death," the future anterior interweaves past and future so tightly that the detective can no longer situate himself in relation to any autonomous temporal dimension. At the end of *Camera Lucida*, Roland Barthes also writes of this death that is at once already behind and still ahead, a death whose temporality he defines by means of the same compound tense, the future anterior. Until his encounter with Alexander Gardner's portrait of Lewis Payne, Barthes had defined the *punctum* as the detail that strikes the viewer above and beyond the average affect of the *studium*. Now, in front of the photograph of a young man awaiting his execution, he discovers another *punctum*, more poignant than any formal detail and common to every photograph—time. Irreducible to any single temporal dimension, the time of the *punctum*, the *punctum* as time, is "an anterior future of which death is the stake,"[9] the simultaneity or intertwining of past and future—"*This will be* and *this has been*," "*that* is dead and *that* is going to die."[10] Facing a photograph, whether or not its subject is still alive at the time of my viewing, I am pierced by the awareness that he or she will have been dead and that I too am already marked by the "catastrophe" of my own future end. Here a function of the photograph's indexicality, rather than of a specific formal arrangement, death in the future anterior nonetheless does not belong to the photographic surface alone nor to its peculiar connection to the referent, but emerges in the domain opened by the encounter between the image and the viewer.

Indeed, it is the emphasis which I place upon this encounter that leads me to discuss the vicissitudes of cinematic vision through an intermingling of media. If I begin each chapter by detour, by addressing questions that pertain to cinema from a site apart from the films—photographs, sculptures, paintings—it is not to overwrite mediatic difference (the indexicality of photography versus the iconicity of painting, the movement of film versus the stillness of photography), but to suggest that cinema gives unique resonance or visibility to a temporality that is not of cinema alone. Writing on the still in film, Raymond Bellour observes that "the projection of one image onto the other, of one state of the image onto another," constitutes a process of temporal displacement that is active, though not identical, in the viewing of both still and moving images—for him, this is the lesson of Holbein's *The Ambassadors*.[11] It is true, Barthes considers film an "illusion" that mimes life, rather than (like photography) a "hallucination" complicit with death.[12] Yet films like *Blow-up* will show us that, under certain formal conditions, cinema too is able to engage its viewer in the temporality of a death out of joint. Even further—that the difference of cinematic temporality lies in the capacity to reveal not only the work of death but "death at work," to foreground the performance of time in its impact on the subject (who is internal to it) and make this performance, in its very unfolding, directly available to the viewer's perception. (Directly but not fully, since the working of death always involves partial blindness and irresolvable obscurity.)

The visibility of this time without ground or now-point, a time of relentless anticipation and retroaction in which both the detective and the spectator are caught, is the subject of my work. Not a history of the transformations undergone by the detective genre, nor a study of the sociocultural factors associated with it, this work is rather the memoir of an encounter. As a writer, I attempt to assume such an experience of time, to repeat in the sphere of language a relationship of vision. If I approach the films indirectly or obliquely, it is to try and partially re-trace their complexity, in a gesture of mimetic desire, rather than simply submit them to analysis. In this respect, Vivian Sobchack's book on the phenomenology of film experience stands as a point of reference. Her conceptualization of cinematic vision as an exchange between "*two* viewing subjects who also exist as visible objects,"[13] has allowed me to think the viewing of film from within the abyss of a "relationality" constituted by the undoing of the subject-object distinction. In the world of perception, we learn from Maurice Merleau-Ponty, this relationality takes the form of a paradoxical reflexivity, which our body most impressively exemplifies: the reversibility between the seer and the seen. As the body can touch only because it is also tangible, the body can only see because it is also visible. However, while Sobchack investigates the reversibility of vision in terms of space and what she calls "the embodied and enworlded eye," I am interested in exploring our enmeshment in the perceptual world as it pertains to time, and to the extent that it involves the (embodied) dissolution of the eye into the world.

In *The Visible and the Invisible*, the phenomenological text that most has informed my work, Maurice Merleau-Ponty invites us to relinquish our desire to hold sway over time—partition it, measure it, and reduce it to autonomous dimensions. Quoting Henri Bergson, he writes that instead "time offers itself to him who wishes only to 'see it,' and who, precisely because he has given up the attempt to seize it, rejoins, by vision, its internal propulsion."[14] All the films under consideration, I will attempt to show, engage this time that resists objectification—a time in radical excess of the present and of any single dimension. Being immersed in it, being captivated by it, the subject finds itself at once constituted and dissolved. If, in *Phenomenology of Perception*, Merleau-Ponty already identifies "time as the subject and the subject as time,"[15] in his last text he returns to time through the notion of "flesh of the world." As "the formative medium of the object and the subject," the flesh is the "stuff" of which all visibles (including our body) are made. Neither mind nor matter, the flesh will allow us to think the time of the films beyond the distinction of subjective, lived time and objective, universal time—Paul Ricoeur's "time of the soul" and "time of the world." In turn, by virtue of their thematic and formal arrangements, the films will lead us to interrogate that which, for Merleau-Ponty, seems to be constantly woven in the fabric of the flesh, inserted in its melodical structure—mortality, existential lack. It is in relation to mortality, to our vulnerability to what exceeds and most profoundly constitutes us, time and the other, that nonchronological, heterogeneous time becomes visible.

Throughout the project, the films assert themselves as more than an occasion for philosophical speculation. There is no hierarchy between them and the philosophical texts they might be supposed to exemplify, rather an erosion of boundaries between what reads and what is read, what thinks and what is thought. "Literature, music, the passions, but also the experience of the visible world are . . . the explorations of an invisible and the disclosure of a universe of ideas"[16]—this invisible and these ideas constituting the other side, the "lining," of a sensible world from which they cannot be disengaged. There is also no hierarchy between the different theoretical discourses I mobilize. As I position myself between phenomenology and Lacanian psychoanalysis, or rather at their crossing, I find that they constitute mutually complicating perspectives rather than separate or competing explanatory principles. For example, if Lacan's split between the eye and the gaze does not coincide with

Merleau-Ponty's distinction between the visible and the invisible, the *Spider's Stratagem* will articulate yet a different phenomenon, weaving a texture in which the chiasm of vision—the intertwining of seeing and being seen—is held by a radical absence or a lack.

The films that guide me through this project are all from the Italian art cinema of the late sixties and early seventies. Some, like Antonioni's *Blow-up* and Pasolini's *Oedipus Rex*, still belong to the so-called golden age of Italian cinema, the period that begins in 1960 with Antonioni's *The Adventure*, Federico Fellini's *La dolce vita* (*The Good Life*), and Visconti's *Rocco e i suoi fratelli* (*Rocco and His Brothers*), and allegedly ends with the changes in Italian culture and society precipitated by 1968. Others, like Antonioni's *The Passenger*, Cavani's *The Night Porter*, and Bertolucci's *The Spider's Stratagem*, appear in a decade, the 1970s, that is already considered of transformation and decline—the period which P. Adam Sitney calls of the second "vital crisis."[17] Despite the canonical periodization, these films constitute for me a cohesive body of work to the extent that, in all of them, the dissolution of the crime scene emerges as a central organizing trope. Of course, postwar Italian cinema—a cinema which I privilege not only for the weight it has in my unconscious memory but also for its recognized tendency to show rather than narrate, to foster perception rather than action—provides other remarkable examples of this dissolution. "A cinema of the seer and no longer of the agent," as Gilles Deleuze admirably demonstrates,[18] neorealism is prefigured by the story of a crime (Visconti's *Obsession*) that ends there where it had begun, tracing a line that folds back upon itself, leaving characters and viewers alike under the spell of the protagonist's dazed look. In this respect, *Obsession* constitutes the direct forerunner of Antonioni's *Cronaca di un amore* (*Story of a Love Affair*, 1950)—both presenting us with a time that deceivingly runs along a straight line, both only returning us to a future that is the reversed image of the past.[19] It is here, I believe, that the dissolution of the crime scene is inaugurated, in this insurgence of perception and time, and if I attempt to explore its manifestations independently of Deleuze's cinema books it is because my point of departure is the phenomenological engrossment of the spectator, of my eye as it expands and contracts in the encounter with the screen.

Together with the works mentioned above, forming a constellation rather than a category, I will also remember Bertolucci's *La commare secca* (*The Grim Reaper*, 1962), *Il conformista* (*The Conformist*, 1971), and *Ultimo tango a Parigi* (*The Last Tango in Paris*, 1972); Marco Bellocchio's *I pugni in tasca* (*Fists in the Pocket*, 1965); Elio Petri's *Indagine su un cittadino al di sopra di ogni sospetto* (*Investigation of a Citizen Above Suspicion*, 1970); Francesco Rosi's *Salvatore Giuliano* (1960) and *Cadaveri eccellenti* (*Illustrious Corpses*, 1975); and Visconti's *Vaghe stelle dell'Orsa* (*Sandra*, 1965). In some cases, the opening scenes already represent a defiant homage to the genre. (*Salvatore Giuliano* begins where the story of Giuliano ends, in the courtyard where the bandit's bullet-riddled corpse is found lying face-down, as the police photograph and describe the details of its position, clothing, and personal effects. *Illustrious Corpses* opens with a Sicilian judge visiting the Cappuchin Crypt, the catacomb that preserves the centuries-old mummies of Palermo's prelates and notables, and then returning to the surface only to be shot to death in full daylight. *Investigation of a Citizen Above Suspicion* draws us into a bourgeois apartment where a barely clothed woman asks the suited man who has just stepped in, "How are you going to kill me this time?"—"Today, I'll cut your throat," he replies, and indeed kills her as anticipated, intentionally leaving behind traces—fingerprints, footprints, a thread from his tie—that should in principle secure his incrimination. He is soon to be identified as the chief inspector of Rome's homicide squad.) In other cases, like in *The Last Tango*, the crime scene proper marks the end rather than the beginning (as Maria Schneider shoots to death the familiar stranger she pretends not to know), or rhythmically returns throughout the film, like in *Fists in the Pocket*, where a middle-class, provincial world is shattered by the violent energy of the young protagonist, who systematically kills his mother and siblings and deliberately refuses the burden of guilt.

While all these films problematize the spatio-temporal parameters of the crime scene—exposing the complicity of power and corruption, reflecting on the process of criminalization, reconfiguring the crime as failure to bear witness, confronting the Oedipal legacy—the films that constitute the focus of this work present us with the most distinct strategies for articulating the future anterior as the time of our enmeshment in cinematic perception, a time of tension rather than repose. I return to them today in the context of a mediatic landscape increasingly obsessed with the image of the crime scene and yet rarely willing to question its conditions of emergence. What defines the contemporary crime scene is often the display of forensic expertise, the demand that everything be made clear and explained in terms of cause and effect, chronological succession, and identifiable agents. Repeatedly, the spectator is faced with scenes that portray (narrativize) the fragility of life and yet is reassured of the fact that, after all, she is still alive—death is what happened to someone else, in a time that is now past. Against this reduction of temporality, I look back at another mode of cinematic engagement and propose a writing of spectatorship that, revolving around description and multiple theoretical infiltrations, attempts to retrace the patterns and rhythms through which each film says or shows that something "will have been."

Chapter 1, "The Scene of the Crime," identifies the crime scene as the site where the interweaving of past, present, and future acquires greatest visibility, taking the form of a death in the future anterior, a death that is simultaneously "already behind" and "still ahead." By drawing upon Lacan's reflection on the gaze and his analysis of *The Ambassadors*, as well as upon the work of Hubert Damisch and Louis Marin, I question the relationship between Renaissance perspective, anamorphosis, and death. I argue that, through a subversive use of perspective, Michelangelo Antonioni's *Blow-up* and *The Passenger* lead us to see death not as a fact but as a possibility, indeed the possibility in relation to which our own capacity for vision is defined. In both films, the crime scene is organized according to the rules of perspective, thus apparently assigning the investigator a position of mastery—at the center of the visual field, yet external to it, he is endowed with the power to survey, measure, and evaluate. However, both films meticulously undermine this structure from within, dramatizing the fact that Albertian perspective contains the principle of its own implosion. Because the viewpoint he occupies corresponds, in terms of projection, to the vanishing point, the beholder finds himself inexorably pulled toward this other infinitesimal place, where things disappear and he will not be able to stand in self-reliance. The return to the crime scene here coincides not with the discovery and ultimate possession of evidence, but with the performance of a double disappearance—the sliding away of image and spectator alike.

In *Blow-up*, the crime scene becomes the site of the constantly deferred, never fully realized encounter between the investigator and the crime. As if it were impossible to see death in the present, the photographer blindly records an event whose significance will only later emerge. A corpse begins to appear after he has transformed the photographic surface into a narrative scenario, metonymically linking a series of details and converting them into a sequence of cinematic shots. Yet, as it reaches its apex, this process of narrativization falls apart. After the detail containing the puzzling image has been enlarged over and over again, what remains is a constellation of grainy particles, a form devoid of narrative value. While it is about to become visible, the corpse retreats again into a state of invisibility, as if there were no stable point between the almost visible and the no longer visible, and visibility could be only imminent or already lost. Similarly, in *The Passenger*, the moment of transition from the living to the dead body is concealed, maintained off-screen through a 360-degree pan that traces a hollow space, installs a void in the center of the scene, and empties out the action from within. The camera, and the spectator with it, sees from this groundless position, this invisible space in which somebody is dying. By the end, death has emerged as a process of disappearance accompanying vision itself, a vanishing always already inscribed in the texture of perception—the inexorable undoing of both the seer and the scene.

Chapter 2, "Desiring Death," explores the intimacy of vision and death as it emerges in Liliana Cavani's *The Night Porter*, a film that represents the return to the crime scene with respect to both the victim's and the aggressor's compulsion to repeat. By reading Leo Bersani's work on masochism together with Lacan's reflection on the circular structure of the drive, I claim that the refusal to bind together that characterizes the death drive can be used to reject standard forms of memory and resist the oblivion realized through the assimilation of marginal perspectives. In *The Night Porter*, it is the rhythm of montage—the intermittent appearance of the so-called flashbacks—that induces the spectator to experience a desire that, in its shattering impact, is productive of images which would not otherwise be visible. Seeing from the point of view of death assumes here the force of a demand—that the past be written through the articulation of new visual forms. Thus, when in the gloomy interiors of postwar Vienna, a former Nazi officer and the woman who had been his favorite prisoner find themselves compelled to resume their sadomasochistic relationship, we witness something other than a simple return of the past. Gradually, as the line separating the active and passive sides of the drive—sadism and masochism, voyeurism and exhibitionism—becomes blurred, a radical contamination of past, present, and future affirms itself. By refusing to let the past be over and done, and choosing to meet their deaths when they still have an alternative, they assume "perverted" positions with respect to the violence of their history, exposing the ambiguous or gray zone they have come to inhabit.

In this chapter, I also question the assumption, laid bare in Cavani's film but often hidden in contemporary discourse, that the survivor of a violent crime will ultimately fulfill her role as witness by testifying in a court of law. In his work on Auschwitz, Giorgio Agamben has cogently argued against this conflation of ethics and law, and the reduction of truth and justice to judgment. It is only as *auctor*, he claims, as creator of a language that at once implicates and exceeds her, that the survivor can bear witness to the past and those who have not survived. Can we think of analysis as another zone of experimentation, a mode of creation other than poetry but in a relation of intimacy with it, in which testimony can be conceived and performed as that which is in excess of any juridical paradigm? Repeatedly, the figure of the analyst has been aligned with that of the detective. Whether it is Carlo Ginzburg writing on the inferential logic that unites Freud, Morelli, and Holmes, or Slavoj Žižek identifying different styles of detection, what is generated is an isomorphic relation between dream and crime scene, symptom and clue, patient and criminal or juridical witness. After the example of *The Night Porter*, I attempt to displace this analogy by envisioning the analyst not as a detective but as a witness—indeed, as the other witness, the witness to the witness of time that the survivor struggles to be.

Chapter 3, "Seeing Time," interrogates the relation between time and the subject of perception through Pier Paolo Pasolini's *Oedipus Rex*, a poetic and eccentric return to what constitutes the archetypal detective story as well as the founding myth of psychoanalysis. By expanding upon the notion of free indirect subjectivity, which Pasolini himself has theorized, and confronting it with the work of Béla Balázs and Merleau-Ponty, I maintain that the film defies the very investigative impetus it is expected to celebrate. There, in a portion of the visible where the detective sees the traces of an event which has already occurred, a scene which is to be analyzed according to uniform spatio-temporal coordinates, Pasolini and his Oedipus see a depth they cannot manipulate. This depth, I argue, is at once of the visible and of time—belonging to what Merleau-Ponty calls "the flesh of the world"—and is most intensely manifested in the encounter between the human face and the landscape. In the prologue, a row of trees is framed by a traveling, almost handheld camera, as if seen through the eyes of the infant who, lying on the grass next to his mother, looks at the surrounding world for the first time. When it reappears, in the epilogue, this mass of green leaves brushing against the sky is no longer the same. It now leads back to the eyes of a grown man, a blind beggar who has lastly returned to the meadow of his infancy. Between the epilogue and the prologue, set in twentieth-century Italy, there unfolds the mythical Greek tale, which begins when a baby with swollen feet is rescued from death, and ends when a sightless and desperate Oedipus is led away from Thebes. Although literally identical, the shots of the trees are separated by a distance that eludes chronological ordering—a memory in excess of the subject, a visual intertwining of past, present, and future through which Oedipus, not the riddle solver but the wanderer, the one who is going to die, is dispersed to the point of dissolution.

The fourth and last chapter, "Twilight," inquires into the truth of the crime scene by following the convoluted thread of Bernardo Bertolucci's *The Spider's Stratagem*. Freely adapted from "The Theme of the Traitor and the Hero," the film embraces Borges's idea of a labyrinth not of space but of time, transferring it from the domain of language to that of perception. Thus, when a man returns to the town where his father, a venerated antifascist hero, was mysteriously assassinated, character and spectator alike are challenged to seek the truth outside the parameters of referential accuracy. But how does one find the truth, and which truth is to be found, in a labyrinth of time and light? As I explore the film's intricate pattern, I elaborate on Lacan's notion of full speech, attempting to reformulate it as a capacity of perception. Full speech coincides with the subject's assumption of a language that refers back to itself, not as it was, but as it "will have been" in the process of producing new significations—a language inhabiting the temporality of the future anterior. It also coincides with the emergence of truth as revelation, as disclosure that is simultaneously concealment. While Lacan does not address the possibility of articulating full speech in the perceptual domain, I draw on Merleau-Ponty's notion of flesh and argue that twilight—the intermingling of light and darkness for which the film's cinematography has been highly praised—is the light, and time, of perceptual full speech. By virtue of its irreducible ambiguity, the chiasm of past and future which the future anterior manifests eventually emerges as the secret shape of time. Enveloped in this light, indeed made of this light, the labyrinth which character and spectator set out to explore "will have become" through the coiling and coiled lines they patiently trace, not as disembodied or external viewers but as seers made of the same light. In the process, questions that have been haunting this work from the beginning return. What is the responsibility facing those who look back and search for the truth, if the past is not simply transpired but returns in the future as it has been transformed by the future itself? Under which conditions does the future anterior affirm a capacity for transformation, instead of causing what has been to blindly survive?

1

The Scene of the Crime

> *Un beau film*: the crime of the good film is the film itself,
> its time and its performance—*its performing of time*. It
> is not by chance that Apollinaire's fascination with
> the new medium is immediately in 1907 the story of a
> murder, the relation of cinema and crime: film is exactly
> a putting to death, the demonstration of "death at
> work" (Cocteau's "la mort au travail").
>
> Stephen Heath[1]

"X Marks the Spot"

"X Marks the Spot"—the title of a photographic album documenting gangland killings in Chicago; the description of a police procedure
that leaves a sign where a dead body was lying, indicating by means of
white chalk, on a surface or ground, the position in which somebody had
died. George Bataille reviews the book in 1930, briefly commenting on
the public's growing fascination with images of violent death.[2] Among
the photographs reproduced, I see the one showing a corpse trapped in
the icy waters of Lake Michigan—a photograph that captures the impossibility of fixing death to the ground. Once the body is retrieved, there
will be no solid surface to support the sign, but only cracked ice and,
later, flowing water. The photograph registers this moment of suspension,
becoming the trace of an impending disappearance—the disappearance
of the body, which is soon to be removed, and of the sign, which could

only be put in its place pointlessly. The photograph inscribes this double disappearance into its own formal arrangement, thus not only anticipating, but also endlessly performing its occurrence. Flattened against the surface of the ice, obliquely framed, the figure of the dead man is at first indistinguishable—a colorless amalgam, a black-and-white stain.[3] Then, a slight change in the angle of vision, the result of chance more than careful scrutiny, brings the body into relief. I can discern the man's hands, his face, even his striped tie—I can make sense of the human form. Yet this form is not a permanent possession of mine. Another imperceptible turn of the head, a prolonged blink, and the body disappears, again dissolving itself into the frozen surface of the lake. I become prey to a composite feeling, a strange mix of wonder and anxiety. My vision is dispersed throughout the plane of the picture, which now coincides with the surface of the lake, and cannot focus on any single point. For a few moments, I cannot even trace this act of looking back to my eyes—I see with my body and my body is dispersed. It is my whole body that meets the corpse and dissolves with it. I am too in the process of vanishing.

"X Marks the Spot," however, does not give me this ambiguous photograph in isolation. On the same page, I see a group of policemen standing next to the gangster's wrecked car, and then clustered around the corpse, on the point of lifting it out of its peculiar tomb. There is even the drawing of a smoking gun, on the lower left side. The photograph is inserted into a chain, a sequence of images that tell a story of murder, detection, investigation. This story holds the figure of the dead man in place for us, forces our eyes to recognize its contours at any time, fixing the continual appearance and disappearance of forms into a moment of static visibility. Even in the photograph depicting the retrieval of the corpse, what is given to us is not an imminent change of forms, but an action in the process of being accomplished. Such a suggestion of narrative development will neutralize the potential for disappearance inherent in the distorted image of the corpse, externalizing it, attributing it to a series of actions to be performed on a body, which would otherwise remain there as a stable point of reference. Visual distortion is tamed, and death secured to the ground. Death, we are told, is the result of a criminal act belonging to the past, an act which proper investigation will prosecute and prevent from being repeated. The photograph is a record—the trace of a death that has already occurred. The other death—the disappearing of forms which awaits us each time we look at the photograph in isolation—is forgotten. I am now composedly in front of the pictures and survey them with curiosity and dismay, my eyes being free to move and yet anchored to the center of the page, where the pictures overlap. I am no longer the one who vanishes.

I cannot but find, in my description of "X Marks the Spot," the echo of Stephen Heath's reflections on narrative space. In *Questions of Cinema*, Heath criticizes the construction of narrative space as the process which maintains the spectator in a centered and immobile position, holding her prisoner of a desire for imaginary plenitude. By means of narrativization, he argues, classical cinema successfully converts the "space" of the frame into a "place" within the story, the "seen" into a "scene," thus reaffirming a perspectival arrangement of vision that assigns the subject a position of exteriority and mastery with respect to the picture. Narrative movement is in effect false movement—the regulation of movement rather than its expansion—constantly returning the spectator to her designated point of view. In front of the photographic sequence telling the story of a long forgotten underworld murder, I have been this spectator.

What has most significantly influenced my description, however, is a statement by painter Willem de Kooning, which Heath quotes extensively and at a crucial point in his argument on the transformation of space into place, but the implications of which he leaves partially unspoken. The statement highlights the fact that, in Renaissance painting, space carried with it a strong narrative impetus: "It was up to the artist to measure out the exact space for a person to die or to be dead already. The exactness of the space was determined or, rather inspired by whatever reason the person was dying or being killed for. The space thus measured out on the original plane of the canvas surface became a 'place' somewhere on the floor."[4] While bringing to the fore the alliance between perspective and narrative with which Heath is concerned, the passage firmly positions the representation of death at the core of this very alliance. Under the rules of Albertian perspective, de Kooning emphasizes, the painter would organize space around a central and irreversible event—somebody's death. That such a mapping of space coincided

with a structuring of time according to linearity and causality is under-
scored by both Heath and Rosalind Krauss, who originally quoted the
passage.[5] The event at the center of the scene, they remark, constituted
the point of arrival for a series of preceding events, as well as the point
of departure for a subsequent series. It emerged as the moment of the
"now," the present which is enclosed between or delimited by past and
future. But both essays fail to discuss de Kooning's insistence on the
mortal nature of such an event. This indifference to textual details is
surprising, especially in view of the fact that Heath's argument unfolds
between the analyses of two films—Alfred Hitchcock's *Suspicion* (1941)
and Nagisa Oshima's *Death by Hanging* (1968)—in which death plays
more than an incidental role.[6]

I cannot but read my description of "X Marks the Spot" as a note
in the margins of this omission. What I want to focus on, in the relation
between perspective and narrative, homogeneous space and chronological time, is the fatal detail of death. As de Kooning characterizes it, the
"place" to which the space of the canvas is reduced is a place in which
somebody is dead or about to die. In the perspectival world, "place" is
a crime scene. That is, the ordering of space according to the laws of
perspective coincides with the gesture of marking an "X" on the ground,
of fixing death to a place on the floor within the representation, where
the viewer is not. Perspective secures death to the ground—gives death
a ground to rest on—while allowing the viewer to subsist, to stand on
her own ground.

While demonstrating that cinema can preserve or challenge the
longstanding complicity between narrative and perspective, Heath's
essay obliquely points at the scene of the crime as the site where such
conformity or resistance are bound to emerge. It is in the site where
mortality becomes visible, I will then claim, that the Renaissance impetus and the process of subject formation accompanying it are most
strongly complied with or defied. But how does cinema undo the scene
of the crime? What does it mean to envision the crime scene against or
in tension with the requirements of perspective? Would there still be a
"scene" to view, if that place on the floor capturing our look and keeping
it oriented were to dissolve? And where would someone die—*who* indeed
would die—in this newly conceived space? Antonioni's *Blow-up* and *The*

Passenger—not the texts where theory finds its illustration, but the texts through which theory itself is rearticulated—envision these questions in ways that are at once highly innovative and profoundly connected to the tradition of perspective. As I return to their famous murder sequences, I will show that the perspectival system is radically undermined there, where it first came into being, in the space where an "X" was drawn— once a place offering itself to view, now a central void or hole around which gazes and movements revolve. If perspective had its analogue in chronological time, Antonioni's spatial arrangements coincide with forms of convoluted time—configurations in which the present cannot be isolated from the past and the future, and death cannot be relegated to a single temporal dimension.

Blow-up: Returning to the Scene of Perspective

I return, at the end of this detour at the beginning of my work, to Michelangelo Antonioni's *Blow-up*. Freely adapted from Julio Cortázar's enigmatic text "Las Babas del Diablo," *Blow-up* has been seen and read, over and over again, by generations of critics, theorists, and historians.[7] Indeed, *Blow-up* cannot stop being read because it can never be fully seen, because—like the corpse and the photographer whose story it tells—it continues to vanish unexpectedly in front of its spectator. It vanishes in the interruptions, the suspensions, the intervals disseminated throughout its closely woven network of gazes. It disappears at the knots where the drive to see is so perfectly inscribed that a reserve of invisibility is finally disclosed. Repeatedly, the spectator cannot see. Like the photographer (David Hemmings) in the film, who is the representative of my look, I find myself in a state of intermittent blindness. I pause on this impossibility of vision—this withdrawal of the visible which organizes the frame and gives montage its rhythm—and wonder how it relates to the crime scene to which the spectator cannot but return.

I know, after repeated viewings, that the answer lies in the encounter of vision and death. Yet, I do not want to search for it by looking directly at what cannot be seen, as if this invisibility were a matter of fact and not of principle, and the persistence of my gaze could force it into its opposite. *Blow-up* itself reminds us that "we cannot look squarely at either death or the sun,"[8] and I would like to follow its indication. Therefore, I will approach the scene of the crime obliquely, by retracing the deceptively straight line the film draws, from the photographer's arrival at the park to his disappearance on a screen of green grass. After the example of Louis Marin, who invites the viewer to look only at what Giorgione's *The Tempest* makes visible, thus searching for the painting's secret in the multiple gazes it secretes,[9] I will attempt to interpret *Blow-up* by describing the heterogeneous and unexpected looks it mobilizes.

Toward the Vanishing Point

The photographer's name is Thomas. We know that he has spent the night in a shelter, taking black-and-white photographs of its dispossessed residents, and part of the morning in his studio, taking color pictures of high-fashion models. He is not amoral, but slightly detached and prone to distraction. During a pause, he has visited an antique store and in vain asked for "landscapes." He is now outside the store, which sits at the edge of a secluded park, in the heart of London. The still camera casually positioned in front of his eyes, his body flexing at different angles, Thomas is taking pictures again. The shot is not unusually composed—the entrance to the park in the background, the photographer in the foreground, drawn toward something which lies outside the boundaries of the frame. It could be the store window, but the way in which his body is oriented makes the match unlikely. The following shot, however, does not show what is being photographed. Against the rules of suture,[10] the object of Thomas's mechanical recording continues to remain invisible to the spectator and will not be recovered as the narrative proceeds. Instead of a reverse shot, *Blow-up* gives us another shot of Thomas photographing the same invisible object. This time, the camera is situated not in front of him but somewhere inside the park, far enough away to make his body appear quite small. We register a sense of discomfort, as if we had been blindfolded for an instant of indefinite duration and, upon regaining sight, found ourselves in a different place. Indeed, we have been unexpectedly displaced—removed from our place, moved across space—by an operation whose simplicity deserves closer examination.

In his essay on narrative space, Heath had warned us against the alliance between perspective and narrative, and the immobilization it imposes on the spectator.[11] In the initial park sequence, however, the spectator finds herself displaced, while the spatial organization of both shots, following the rules of perspective, had distinctly assigned her a position of masterly overview. The attempt to make sense of this apparent contradiction, which seems to involve more than an ordinary disarticulation of the shot–reverse shot formation, leads me to complicate Heath's account of perspective, introducing historical differentiation into a paradigm that too often is assumed to be homogeneous.[12] The possibility arises that perspective might allow for a greater degree of mobility than Heath recognizes, and the scene of the crime conceived under its rule might not always aim at the regulation of death and the subject's desire.

In the influential essay "The Gaze and the Glance," Norman Bryson distinguishes between two ages of perspective—the epoch of the vanishing point, characterized by the Albertian *costruzione legittima*, and a later epoch, marked by the works of painters such as Titian and Vermeer. Both ages were dominated by the "logic of the Gaze" and the will to reduce the viewing subject to a point, a disembodied and static eye, which in a moment existing outside the flow of time, could contemplate the world without blinking.[13] However, Bryson emphasizes, the epoch of the vanishing point would ultimately fail to realize such a project of reduction, as demonstrated by Raphael's *Marriage of the Virgin*. That painting, with its highly structured architectural space, defines lines of force along which the viewer is invited to travel, to move as an embodied being toward that point on the horizon where things disappear. There is, in fact, a precise equivalence between point of view and vanishing point—as Brunelleschi's first experiment demonstrates, the receding lines forming a fan pattern on the picture plane correspond to the rays of the visual pyramid whose apex is the beholder's eye.[14] In a later essay, Bryson defines the vanishing point as the place "where the viewer does not and cannot exist," "where, *par excellence*, the viewer is not."[15] Yet, it is toward this point that she is drawn by every line crossing the arcades, windows, and pavements of the piazza, in an experience which is as inevitable as it is profoundly disorienting:

The moment the viewer appears and takes up position at the viewpoint, he or she comes face to face with another term that is the negative counterpart to the viewing position: the vanishing point. . . . The self-possession of the viewing subject has built into it, therefore, the principle of its own abolition: annihilation of the subject as center is a condition of the very moment of the look.[16]

Facing the geometric arrangement of the scene, the beholder stands in a position of composed mastery—at the center of the visual field, yet external to it, she is endowed with the power to survey, measure, and evaluate. Yet, because the viewpoint she occupies coincides, in terms of projection, with the vanishing point,[17] she also finds herself pulled toward this other infinitesimal place, where things disappear and she will not be able to stand in self-reliance.

If we look again at the first shot depicting Thomas outside the park, we notice that the scene is arranged according to the parameters of Albertian perspective. Although the setting is not urban, the space resembles that of the piazza—the road and the isolated buildings define multiple lines of flights traveling toward an indefinite point among the trees, on the other side of the entrance to the park. It is from a site which approximates this receding point that the second shot is taken, as though the camera had moved along the centric ray extending from the viewpoint to the vanishing point and placed itself close to the latter, inside the park. There is no arbitrariness in the choice of this spot—the orthogonal lines now crossing the paved trails and the aligned trees converge toward the site of the initial viewpoint, the place where Thomas stands. With geometric precision the second shot creates a scene that is the reversal of the previous one, but not in the sense associated with the shot–reverse shot formation. Instead of concerning itself with the object of the character's look, this kind of reversal isolates and brings to the foreground the ocular activity of the spectator in her identification with the camera rather than with the character.[18] To the spectator, it offers a dramatization of the mutual implication of viewpoint and vanishing point—an introduction to the surprises awaiting those who walk a reversed path.

The sequence is important not despite but by virtue of its brief duration. In provoking a sense of disorientation, it anticipates, at the level of the enunciation, what will gradually emerge in the course of the film—that perspective contains the principle of its own implosion, and the centric ray, which Alberti had named "the prince of rays," "the most active and the strongest of all the rays,"[19] constitutes the site of a reversal capable of diffusing the beholder's scopic mastery. However, because of its brevity, the sequence alters our mood but leaves us uncertain about the reasons of this change. We do not know what has occurred—we have not had the time to see clearly, analyze, ascertain this surprising reversal of perspective.[20]

Abruptly transferred to a diametrically opposite standpoint, we have the distinct impression of being watched but we do not know by whom. On the one hand, we feel as if we were still there where Thomas is, taking pictures, and somebody were monitoring us. Since the separation of primary and secondary identification has positioned the spectator in two places at the same time—"here" with the camera, and "over there" with the character—it is possible to suggest that I (as character) am being watched by myself (as camera). On the other hand, while occupying the new viewpoint, which lies close to what had previously been the vanishing point, we sense that someone else is here, further behind us or perhaps all around, a stranger whom we cannot see but whom we can perceive, as we perceive the sound of leaves rustling in the wind. Who is this other watching us from a position of uncanny proximity and irreducible alterity? In his seminal work on perspective, Hubert Damisch claims that "the vanishing point . . . functioned, within the limits of the painting, . . . as the semblance of an eye,"[21] that is, as the equivalent of the beholder's point of view, but also specifies that the two could not be conflated.[22] Then, if the vanishing point functions as an eye and yet is more than the mirror image of the viewpoint, to whom does this other eye, which I cannot incorporate into my own, belong? As we are about to enter the park, we experience a peculiar kind of suspense, a sense of diffuse anxiety, which only later will fall upon the character.

"The One Who Looks Is Never Discreet"

The park is secluded and peaceful. On the top of a small hill, we see an open space or clearing,[23] delimited by a picket fence and thick bushes and interrupted by a few trees. The trees and the fence are arranged to form lines of flight converging on the horizon, where a compact and indistinct mass of green stands in isolation. A young woman (Vanessa Redgrave) and a man with gray hair are walking on the grass, traversing the clearing in the direction of this distant point. The woman is pulling the man, who seems to pose some resistance. Their movement is restrained and inexorable, as if the result of silently antagonistic forces. Eventually, they kiss and embrace. As in the initial park sequence, the space resembles that of the piazza, and Thomas, who is now taking pictures of the couple while hiding behind the fence, occupies the site from which a masterly overview of the scene can be enjoyed. He is the unseen watcher, Sartre's voyeur at the keyhole, separated from the spectacle by an opaque layer which only the viewfinder can pierce. At the level of the enunciation, however, two shots of Thomas taken from an impossible camera position—a point high above the ground and on the side of the unaware couple—disturb the perspectival arrangement of the visual field, reviving the spectator's sense of confusion and anticipating the events to come.

For a long time silence permeates the scene. We hear only the wind and the rustling of leaves, punctuated by the metallic click of the camera. Then, the watcher is caught in the act of watching, not by a third party behind his back, but by the one who is being watched. The woman circumspectly interrupts the embrace and, after a few moments of hesitation, rushes toward Thomas, who in turn runs away. The reversal in the visual field is conspicuous. By inspecting the space unfolding in front of her and moving along a path which coincides with the scene's centric ray, the woman becomes the figure of a conversion that reorients all the lines of force and positions the photographer on the passive side of the viewfinder. However, unlike Sartre's voyeur, Thomas is not overcome with shame. When the woman confronts him, covering her face and crying, "Stop, stop . . . you can't photograph people like that," he responds by photographing her at close range, stating, "Who says I can't—some people are bullfighters, some people are politicians, I am a photographer." That is, he dismisses the fact that another person's look has transformed him into a picture and aggressively reaffirms his position as point of view. After refusing to hand over his film, Thomas even goes back to the clearing, now deserted, and takes a few last pictures of the green expanse and of the woman, who by tracing backward the path along which she had previously moved, eventually disappears on the horizon.

Thomas's determination can hardly be overemphasized. In its unapologetic tone, it brings to the fore the connection between seeing according to the laws of perspective and the drive to see—that peculiar imbrication of vision and desire which, Damisch points out, has characterized the perspectival system from the very beginning:

> If the one who looks is never "discreet" (*benché chi guarda ogni volta non sia discreto*), this is because, in the conditions applying to vision under the perspective rule, he is always a *voyeur*. . . . If perspective is a "scabrous" thing, as one reads in Filarete, . . . it is primarily because it appeals, in the subject, to the scopic drive, pretending to reduce it—Brunelleschi's experiments have no other meaning—to the function and status of a witness, if not—once again—of a *voyeur*.[24]

The passage leaves no doubts—the one who resides at the viewpoint is a voyeur, a subject occupying a position of scopic mastery. However, the passage also distinctively suggests that the subject does not autonomously seize but is assigned to this active position. It is perspective, as a system in excess of any one of its points, that places the subject at the apex of the visual pyramid coinciding with the eye. It is the same system that impinges upon the subject's drive to see, "pretending" to confine it within the boundaries of voyeurism. The term *pretending* is crucial here, because it points to a flaw at the heart of the system, a potentially lethal imperfection, which the system conceals in full view. If the subject in Brunelleschi's experiments is a voyeur, Damisch specifies, he is indeed "a singular kind of voyeur, one who discovers that he is himself being looked at."[25] We begin to perceive such an imperfection in the initial park sequence, when the film confronts us, the spectators of the scene, with the sudden reversal between point of view and vanishing point. We detect it again when the woman turns around and runs toward the photographer—although, in this case, the presence of another human being on the side opposite the viewpoint seemingly decreases the inversion's disorienting effect. Now that Damisch has highlighted a scenario in which vision is thoroughly permeated with desire, these reversals, together with the imperfection they indicate, assume a new density. Beyond the "pretense" of perspective, there emerges the threat or promise of a subject that exceeds the eye or point of view—a subject that cannot be relegated to the active side of the scopic drive.

In *The Four Fundamental Concepts of Psychoanalysis*, Jacques Lacan analyzes the imbrication of vision and desire toward which Damisch has directed our attention, and unrelentingly questions the privileges ascribed to the subject of perspective. Indeed, it is by posing a split between the eye and the gaze—the punctiform seeing of the subject and the encompassing vision of what he calls the gaze—that Lacan is able to integrate vision into the domain of desire, thus adding the scopic drive to the list of drives.[26] *Blow-up* repeatedly shows us how difficult it is to make such a split visible. As spectators, we are given a glimpse of it while lingering at the edge of the park, observing its evaporation when the contingent, personal gaze of the woman confronts Thomas's voyeuristic intrusion, and we witness its definitive appearance through Antonioni's groundbreaking depiction of the crime scene. However, at the end of the second park sequence, we find ourselves in a remarkable position. By the time Thomas leaves the park with his negatives, the scene of the crime that *Blow-up* invents for us is "already behind" and "still ahead." Both character and spectator have already encountered it but have failed to recognize its shape in the immediacy of the present.

I would like to take advantage of this peculiar accident, this blindness of the seeing eye, which has so discretely afflicted photographer and viewer alike, and pause on Lacan's analysis of the split between the eye and the gaze. The dangers of perspective—the limitations but also the challenges that the perspectival system poses to the subject—find in Lacan one of the most thought-provoking interpreters. I will read his analysis in light not only of Damisch's and Bryson's works but also in relation to *Blow-up* itself. The order of presentation notwithstanding, the film always moves me to reread the theoretical text and not vice versa.

The Split Between the Eye and the Gaze

In the seminars collected under the rubric "Of the Gaze as *Objet Petit a*," Lacan presents his conceptualization of the visual field through the support of triangulated diagrams. The first diagram, that of the eye, describes the ideal of Renaissance perspective: the subject stands at the apex of the triangle, in the invisible position of the "geometral point," while the "object" is placed at the far wall, in full view. Halfway between them, on a line parallel to that of the wall, there is a transparent "image," in all respects similar to the window adopted by Alberti as a metaphor for the canvas. The second diagram, that of the gaze, inverts the first one: no longer invisible, the subject now occupies the site of the "picture," at the far wall of the triangle, and is exposed to a gaze which Lacan defines as "point of light" and locates at the apex. As picture, the subject appears through the mediation of a "screen," which runs in the middle section of the triangle as the image did in the first diagram but, unlike the image, is utterly opaque. The third diagram, which elucidates the relation between eye and gaze, is obtained by superimposing the two previous triangles in inverted form. The point of light is now aligned with the object, while the geometral point appears at the site of the picture, and in between them, image and screen have come to coincide.

This new, composite figure constitutes, in its very structure, the graphic trace of an irreducible ambiguity—in the visual field, the subject who looks at the world from the perspectival viewpoint is always also looked at from a point of radical alterity. This point, which lies outside the subject and yet constitutes him at the most profound level, must not be confused with any contingent, local, personal point of view. Lacan relentlessly emphasizes the radical dissymmetry between eye and gaze—between the punctual, embodied character of the former and the diffuse, impersonal quality of the latter. "I see only from one point," he writes, "but in my existence I am looked at from all sides."[27] The effect is utterly decentering. In the field of the gaze, the subject of vision emerges on the passive side of the scopic drive—he is first and foremost a picture, a multiplicity of pictures, taken by a point of light. Indeed, Lacan defines the gaze as "the instrument through which light is embodied and through which . . . I am *photo-graphed*,"[28] thus reversing the metaphor of the camera, often adopted to demonstrate the privileges of the perspectival eye, and suggesting that the subject of vision finds himself at the passive end of the viewfinder. Nobody, however, seems to be at the other end, if not light itself—the gaze is the instrument rather than the agent, the camera rather than the photographer.

While irreducible, the split between the eye and the gaze can nonetheless be masked or obfuscated. In the domain of geometral perspective, something like "an elision of the gaze" occurs,[29] and the subject is granted a position which claims to incorporate the attributes of the all-seeing gaze. At the center of a homogeneous, abstract, rationalized space, the perspectival subject coincides with the Cartesian subject of thought.

He occupies the point from which perception originates and unfolds as if light were a thread or straight line linking his eye to the object. This model of vision, Lacan points out, would work even if the subject were blind, since it realizes a structuring of space and not of sight. Here the subject apprehends the objects of perception in the form of representations and relates to them according to that "*belong to me* aspect of representations so reminiscent of property."[30] This is the same proprietary relationship that the ego, and not the fully symbolic subject, entertains with its mirror image. By investing his situated, embodied, limited look with the attributes of the all-seeing gaze, the subject of geometral perspective affirms the ego's aspiration to mastery and knowledge, subtracting things from the flow of becoming, and grounding himself in a state of misrecognition, a condition of imaginary plenitude.

The subject which concerns Lacan, however, is in radical excess of any egoic structure. If the voyeur at the keyhole can be surprised by the irruption of the gaze into his perceptual field, this is because he is ultimately other than the Cartesian subject of thought. "Is it not clear," writes Lacan, "that the gaze intervenes here only in so much as it is not the annihilating subject, correlative of the world of objectivity, who feels himself surprised, but the subject sustaining himself in a function of desire?"[31] Significantly, at this point in the seminar on anamorphosis, the gaze takes on an auditory quality. By focusing on those elements in Sartre's text that are not visual—footsteps suddenly heard in a corridor, the sound of rustling leaves in the countryside—Lacan reaffirms the impossibility of conflating the gaze as such with the look of a personalized other. For Lacan, "the gaze I encounter . . . is, not a seen gaze, but a gaze imagined by me in the field of the Other."[32] However, unusual circumstances—the opaque brilliance of dreams, a strangely autonomous object, a detail on a pictorial surface—might lead this imagined gaze to emerge at the level of the scopic register.

When the space of Hans Holbein's *The Ambassadors*—a space constructed according to geometral laws and inhabited by symbols of knowledge and social privilege—is disrupted by the appearance of a distorted skull, the split between the eye and the gaze becomes visible. By virtue of anamorphosis and its reversed use of perspective, the spectator who looks at the painting from a lateral position witnesses the implosion of geometral optics and finds herself in a decentered, expanded field. She realizes not only that her look cannot be conflated with the gaze, but also that the gaze is outside, on the side of the painting, that someone or something other than herself possesses it, and that she is a being who is looked at. Indeed, the anamorphic ghost doubly defies the Cartesian subject's sense of mastery. Not only does it sever the look from its illusory identification with the gaze, but it also reveals that the gaze was called to fill a lack which is ultimately connected with human finitude and death. The sudden interjection of the skull shatters the ambassadors' frozen composure, reminding the observer of a time when she will be dead.

If the nature of the enigmatic object at the bottom of the canvas is most relevant, so is the time of its appearance. As he approaches the secret of Holbein's painting, Lacan emphatically asks: "What . . . is this object, which from some angles appears to be flying through the air, at others to be tilted? You cannot know—for you turn away, thus escaping the fascination of the picture. Begin by walking out of the room in which no doubt it has long held your attention. It is then that, turning around as you leave . . . you apprehend in this form . . . What? A skull."[33] In offering a delayed answer, the passage reproduces a certain duration, the temporal interval which elapses between the viewer's fascination with the enigmatic shape and her eventual identification of the skull. Obliquely positioned in the lower center of the canvas, floating just above the ground, the death's head is not fully nor permanently there. It appears in relation to a movement which involves the beholder's physicality—a last-minute turn, a double take from the edge of the room. Always on the verge of revealing its contour and yet always ready to retreat into the indistinct, the skull exists in a state of precarious visibility. The subject of vision mobilized by The Ambassadors partakes of this instability. While the perspectival eye is supposed to see clearly and in the immediacy of the present, the anamorphic viewer sees in time and through zones of blindness, moved by the desire to incessantly return to a glimmering distortion that she cannot ignore and cannot translate into a static figure.[34]

Lacan himself returns to Holbein's painting. After introducing the triangulated schemas of the eye and the gaze, he pauses again on anamorphosis, qualifying it as "a use of the geometral dimension" which allows vision to lure the viewer into the picture and represent her as trapped there. Indeed, such a redefinition marks a shift of emphasis in Lacan's discourse that is crucial for our analysis—the perspectival system, previously exposed as partial and inadequate with respect to what vision has to offer, now emerges as the site of latent possibilities. "For us," Lacan states, "the geometral dimension enables us to glimpse how the subject who concerns us is caught, manipulated, captured, in the field of vision."[35] From this new angle of observation, anamorphosis makes use of a potential for subversion that is already inscribed in the order of perspective. After all, the diagram of the gaze perfectly counters the one of the eye. If perspective can be dismantled by the appearance of the gaze on the side of the object, this is because the gaze has been hidden there, from the outset, in the form of the vanishing point. Bryson proposes a similar interpretation when, in his analysis of Raphael's *Marriage of the Virgin*, he defines the vanishing point as "a black hole of otherness,"[36] and then proceeds to tease out the similarities between such a pictorial example and Lacan's story of the sardine can and his reading of *The Ambassadors*. However, what Bryson does not say is that, whenever the split between the eye and the gaze becomes visible, a temporality emerges in radical excess of instantaneity. It takes more than the blink of an eye for the viewer to travel toward the vanishing point, along the path marked by the painting's lines of force, or to identify the enigmatic shape at the bottom of an otherwise transparent picture. Does this suggest that the fissure of eye and gaze can be seen only in retrospect or in anticipation, as though it always belonged to another time, a time out of joint? It is not by chance that *Blow-up* delineates a crime scene which is at once "already behind" and "still ahead" with respect to its spectator.

"I Have Not Had Time to See"

Thomas's studio is a loft built on multiple levels and without any clear distinction between working and living areas. In this space, whose layout is never made clear to the viewer, Thomas embarks on the laborious process of developing, analyzing, and enlarging the pictures he took in the seemingly orderly space of the park. He is now driven by the suspicion that he suffered from a loss of vision, but that what he did not see must have been recorded by his camera. While such a suspicion might express the determination to consider the camera as a more powerful eye—an eye endowed with the attributes of the all-seeing gaze and thus capable of restoring perspective's fictitious stability—the ensuing investigation will repeatedly expose the radical fissure between eye and gaze, together with the complex temporality of its emergence. The very process in which Thomas engages, with its relentless production of fragmented and enlarged images, is from the beginning closer to the logic of the Glance rather than the Gaze. According to Bryson, the latter is "subject to two great laws: the body (of the painter, of the viewer) is reduced to a single point, the *macula* of the retina surface; and the moment of the Gaze (for the painter, for the viewer) is placed outside duration."[37] The studio sequences, however, offer us a viewer whose corporeal being is fully invested in the labor of vision (assuming different postures, touching the prints, and making use of marker and magnifying glass), and whose seeing exceeds the instantaneity of the eye blink. Not only does it take him time to travel along the scene's lines of flight and reach the vanishing point, but time cannot be reduced to a linear succession of instants, as the extraordinary montage sequences render it visible.

After developing the negatives, Thomas sets his investigation in motion by selecting and assembling two photographs, as though vision were not so dissimilar from language and also required a play of differences.[38] For several moments his look, which the camera aligns with ours, shifts back and forth between the two images—on the left, the woman pulling her companion; on the right, their embrace at the center of the clearing. Finally, in the second picture, a detail is isolated and highlighted—the woman's anxious look, which seems to hold, in its full visibility, the secret of the invisible object it intends. Thomas punctiliously follows the look he has magnified, tracing its trajectory all the way to the bush on the far right, behind the fence. Here, amid the foliage, another detail seizes his attention and, as he progressively enlarges what is at first only a strange gleam, almost a stain of light, the contours of a gun and a silencer take shape. On the basis of this last detail, the entire series of photographs, which in the meantime he has printed and arranged in a line, is retroactively endowed with sense and directionality. The woman leads the man to an agreed site and apprehensively turns toward the spot where she knew the assassin was hiding. Then she hears some unexpected sounds, turns around to scan the surroundings, hesitating for an instant, and finally catches sight of the photographer—who she chases, leaving the man alone. As Thomas reaches the end of the series, he believes he has saved the man's life.

At first sight, the narrative impetus permeating *Blow-up*'s most celebrated sequence does not escape Heath's critical account of the alliance between perspective and narrative. "What gives the moving space its coherence in time, decides the metonymy as a 'taking place,'" Heath writes regarding classical continuity, "is here 'the narrative itself,' and above all as it crystallizes round character as look and point of view."[39] In the course of his optical investigation, Thomas relentlessly transforms the photograph's surface into a narrative, metonymically linking a series of details and converting them into a sequence of cinematic shots whose meaning is constructed in relation to his point of view. As if spatial perspective had its temporal analogue in linear succession, the depth of the scene is translated in a chain of consecutive events, the flawless montage reinstating the unity which the proliferation of details had seemingly dissolved. At the end, "the spectator must see,"[40] that is, must find the object capable of satisfying the very desire which the film had initially frustrated. The narrative thrust, as organized around the character's point of view, is so unremitting that even the image of the shiny object behind the fence, in its anamorphic distortion, is finally turned into the stable shape of a firearm—the phallic ghost becoming the very object that ostensibly allows the montage sequence to reach its completion and vision to regain its plenitude. The suspicion arises that we might be facing a gigantic operation of suture.

Upon closer inspection, it distinctly emerges that *Blow-up*'s most famous sequence does not submit to but, rather, plays with the idea of narrative space. The relay between the woman's look and the gun—the long sought-after eye-line match which brings together all the pieces of the puzzle—is not invisibly composed but manifestly enacted in the three-dimensional space of the studio, the photographer using the ninety-degree angle formed by two walls to stage the optical encounter.[41] Most importantly, neither this relay nor the ensuing storyline exhausts the visual possibilities of the photographic series, that is, in Heath's terms, successfully converts the space of the frame, the "seen" into a self-enclosed "scene." At each juncture the film counters its own narrative impulse by lingering on the surface of the prints, thus revealing forms and shades rather than imminent or past actions. Because both character and camera never occupy a fixed position in relation to the photographs, the whole sequence is pervaded by a strange, internal instability. "Setting the viewing point into motion," Marin writes on the topic of Dutch painting, "displaces not only the site of vision, but also the framing and the distance and, from then on, the very object of the gaze, the 'hidden' spectacle, distanced from the world accessible to the eye, is dispersed."[42] As if the descriptive mode of Northern art had been intermingled with the narrative, theatrical mode of Albertian perspective, each detail loses its unity and self-evidence, making itself available for indefinite narrative development. Accordingly, though the relay between the woman's look and the gun ultimately allows the viewer to construct "a single, oriented sense," each glance at the photographic surface can, at some point, intend more than one object, thus generating plural, contradictory story lines.[43] The network of glances traversing the frame makes visible a time that is repeated, interfered with, punctured, and multiplied from within. If *Blow-up* defines a narrative scenario, it does so in terms of "the labyrinth of the straight line" that Borges envisioned.[44]

Almost responding to this excess of vision, this trap set for the eye, Thomas returns to the two photographs at the end of the series—the one showing the park, now deserted, in its serene perspectival arrangement; the other recording the woman's last halt, next to the bush toward which converge the scene's lines of force. Once more, the analyst oscillates between two images, until a detail seizes his attention—this time, an opaque stain on the ground, protruding from the bush in the far center. As he enlarges the puzzling detail, the uncertain shape of a corpse begins to appear and, together with it, the threat of a different narrative closure—he did not save the man's life but blindly captured his death. Yet, on the verge of reaching its apex, the newly revived process of narrativization falls apart. After the image is magnified one more time, what remains is a constellation of grainy particles, a blown-up stain, a picture devoid of narrative value. "If we concentrate on a detail—the hand of the painter, for example, in the *Art of Painting*," Svetlana Alpers writes on the art of describing in the Nordic tradition, "our experience is so vertiginous because of the way the hand is assembled out of tone and light without declaring its identity as a hand."[45] This is the vertigo into which Thomas and the spectator fall—"the vertigo of the stain," the dizziness provoked by a figure at the limits of form, a figure sliding away toward the indistinct and the inorganic.[46] Not yet or no longer clearly identifiable as a corpse, such a figure cannot constitute a fixed term in the last eye-line match that Thomas attempts to arrange. While it is about to become visible, the corpse retreats again into a state of invisibility, as if there were no stable point between the almost visible and the no longer visible, and as if visibility could be only imminent or past. At the end, the picture of the gun intends an object that does not exist in the present.

Like Holbein's anamorphic skull, the corpse subsists only as the marker of an unrecordable moment, the impossible trace of a missing time. What Thomas, who represents my look, could not see that morning in the park, and still cannot see after his painstaking reconstruction, is the moment of death. As he sits in his studio, caught between the picture of the gun and the enlargements of the dissolving corpse, the before and the after of the murder, he realizes that he will always have been too early or too late for that instant of shattering penetration, when the bullet meets the man's body. We see here a temporal configuration similar to the one that Louis Marin delineates in his admirable analysis of the *Martyrdom of Saint Blaise*, in the Chapelle des Moines, Berzé-la-Ville, France. This fresco, painted long before the invention of perspective, shows the beholder not the decapitation itself but its two demarcating moments—the saint's head falling onto the ground, the executioner raising his sword to perform the lethal cut. The instant of death emerges as the ineradicable yet invisible hiatus between them. Marin's words lead us through this time in radical excess of the present:

What thus eludes my gaze, and its attentive contemplation, on this late September afternoon, which gathers in the painted work in peaceful admiration, is precisely what, for it, will "always already" have taken place: that flash of death. . . . In that interval where my gaze falls into the vertigo of the story, a power of seeing is exhausted, that of grasping the event through representation, and in this endless loss, the subject goes through the test of time at the point of a gaze that meets nothing. For what it ought to have recognized is forever past without ever having been seen; what it ought to have encountered is forever missed. The subject will always have been late to this meeting, this encounter with a cut, the chopping off of a head that has already rolled. A measureless measure of this test of time. "I have not had time to see. I shall never have had time to see: I shall forever lack that time.". . . Before the torture of Saint Blaise represented by the Roman painter, by losing his gaze in the invisibility of death at the very instant of death, the subject experiences himself in his temporal destination, proves to himself, even if in anguish, the infinite virtuality of his end.[47]

Caught between the anticipation and the memory of death, the past and the future of an instant which, in the space of the representation, can exist only as trace, the viewer can no longer relegate death to a place or a time other than where and when she stands. Because there is no place for death in the present, death is now, for her, that which will always have been, the inevitability of her own effacement.

We face, at this point, what seems to be the opposite of the per-spectival scene—a space in which "death cannot take place, cannot have a place,"[48] as opposed to the narrative space described by de Kooning, organizing itself around the spot on the floor where someone dies. If the perspectival scene coincides with this staging of death as an objective and fully visible event, the fresco produces a mise-en-abyme that shatters spatial and temporal perspective alike. However, if the vanishing point is "the anchor of a system which *incarnates* the viewer,"[49] inviting her to move along the lines of flight converging on the horizon, it is also the guarantee of her disappearance—a threat or promise of invisibility already embedded, structurally and through projection, in the point of view itself, as a constitutive hollow or void. At the vanishing point, to-ward which the spectator is inexorably driven, *Blow-up* installs a magni-fied stain, the not yet or no longer identifiable image of a corpse. In this image, Thomas sees not the dead body he will be, but the dead body he will always have been, in a circularity of past and future which offers no escape, the time of appearance of the corpse being isomorphic with the time of the death it exposes—death in the future anterior.

In *Blow-up*, what intermittently appears at the vanishing point, where the clarity of the scene should be stretched into infinity, is the

brilliant opacity of the stain, in which the gaze becomes visible.[50] Caught
in this impossible identification with the gaze, the spectator experiences
not merely the dismantling of optical mastery but the dissolution of
vision itself. Death emerges, not as a moment of blindness belonging to
the future, but as a process of disappearance accompanying vision from
within, a sliding away inscribed in the texture of perception from the beginning. What is this fading into invisibility of seen and seer alike? What
kind of desire does it express? The attempt to answer these questions will
lead me to my final detour.

The Passenger: Vanishing

The Hotel de la Gloria is a white, one-story building in rural Spain,
where, at the end of *The Passenger*, those looking for David Locke (Jack
Nicholson), a television journalist who was believed to be dead, and
those hunting for Robertson, an arms dealer who is believed to be still
alive, almost meet, missing each other by only a few minutes. During
this crucial interval, which the camera makes visible through a long, continuous tracking shot, a man will die the death of another—his own
death as another. In a different hotel, at the beginning of the film, Locke
had exchanged his identity with that of a man he barely knew.[51] Upon
returning from a failed reportage, Locke had found Robertson (Charles
Mulvehill) lifeless, whereupon, taking advantage of their uncanny physical resemblance, he had proceeded to switch clothes, passports, and
personal belongings. Dead to his wife and colleagues, he had followed
the path traced in advance by his double and kept appointments he had
never made. He is now at the Hotel de la Gloria, the last meeting place
in Robertson's appointment book and a further promise of involvement
in the Third World events he used to film as a reporter. With him is the
young woman (Maria Schneider), who, after a repeated chance encounter, has become his traveling companion and lover.

As the journey comes to an end, Locke seems to retreat from vision,
and the camera affirms its radical autonomy from the characters' point
of view. Twice, as the woman stands near the window, Locke remains
at a distance and asks her, "What can you see?" Twice, without moving,
she describes casual activities, disparate gestures, and the dust. In both

cases, the camera doubles or splits the subject as well as the object of vision—the first shot showing the seer only as a mirror image, the second one revealing the spectacle from a stance which does not coincide with the seer's viewpoint. Then, moving close to Locke and running a finger along his profile, the woman remarks, "Isn't it funny . . . all the shapes we make?"[52] To this understated celebration of worldly forms, Locke replies by telling the story of a man who regained his sight after forty years of blindness. The initial elation, the uncontainable joy he felt at all the faces, the colors, the landscapes the world had to offer, was soon superseded by disappointment and fear. The world could not but look poorer than he had imagined, full as it was of unexpected dirt and ugliness. He ended up living in the dark, afraid and alone, until he killed himself. As the story comes to an end, the camera abandons the couple for a few moments, traveling upward and pausing on a framed landscape or view, an insignificant and yet slightly haunting portrait of nature—not the wonderful object capable of filling the void that sight has brought to our eyes, but the reminder of other views and other landscapes we will have missed forever.

After the woman exits the room, leaving Locke lying on the bed, the film's penultimate shot begins—a seven-minute-long tracking shot that lasts for as long as it takes for a man to be left alive and found dead, and for the camera to travel the distance between the viewpoint and the vanishing point of the perspectival scene. Positioned inside the room, opposite the window overlooking the courtyard, the camera is now the eye of no one, and yet it becomes the spectator's only anchorage or standpoint. As the camera slowly moves toward the outside, the cinematic frame comes to coincide with the window, and then with increasingly smaller portions of it, thus producing a magnifying effect not dissimilar from the one encountered in *Blow-up*, and equally conducive to an intermingling of description and narration. Through the window, opened onto the courtyard and yet traversed by thick, simple bars, a scene unfolds that finds its center in an old man who is sitting alongside a decrepit arena, there as the substitute vanishing point in a view whose horizon is blocked by a wall.[53] As the camera continues to move forward, people and things intermittently cross the dusty courtyard, inscribing the ground with multiple, intersecting lines—the diegetic equivalent of the chiasmatic figure the enunciation is about to trace.[54] We see the woman pacing the courtyard, a boy pestering the man on the chair, two men getting out of a white Citroen and silently going off in separate directions. One will remain outside and divert the woman's attention from the window, the other will head toward the hotel. We do not see him entering the building or Locke's room, but we hear the sound of a door, very close to us, opening and closing, and another, louder noise. By the time the car drives away, the woman is standing at the vanishing point, next to the old man, and we are about to advance through the bars. After accomplishing this impossible passage, the camera interrupts its forward movement (inside-to-outside) and substitutes for it a circular pan (left-right), wide enough to track the arrival of two police cars. Finally, while the woman, Locke's wife, and the detectives rush into the hotel, it stops at the entrance and slides alongside the white wall, until it reaches the barred window previously left behind. Now positioned in the courtyard, it is ready to record the discovery of Locke's lifeless body, having performed, with a 360-degree turn, a complete reversal of inside and outside.[55]

Like *Blow-up*, *The Passenger* affirms the impossibility of seeing the crime in the present. Here, the moment of transition from the living to the dead body is concealed, maintained off-screen by means of a complex camera movement that traces a hollow space, installing a void in the center of the scene—in the process, vision is emptied from within. The camera, along with the spectator, sees from this groundless position, this invisible space in which somebody is dying. Through a complete reversal of perspective, the vanishing point, the point sanctioning the disappearance of the scene, is projected all the way back to the viewpoint and even behind it. As Damisch notices, "The vanishing point is not an image—narrowly constructed, a geometric image—of the point of view . . . it will on the contrary be thrown far behind the image of the observer, who will have it, so to speak, *at his back*—or, to use Pascal's language, 'behind his head.'"[56] Ahead of me as the scene's vanishing point, but also behind my head as its projection, death occurs but does not "take place" in the sense defined by de Kooning and Heath—its space being in excess of any "X" marking a spot on the ground, its time coinciding not with the instant of the gunshot but with the duration of the shot, if not of the entire film. Death is where I "am" in a time that is not the present—where I will have been.

The undoing of the crime scene coincides here with the enactment of a crisscrossing, a chiasmatic reversal that affects both space and time. Slowly and yet inexorably led along a circular trajectory, the spectator becomes the witness of a death that she cannot see, an event that is "behind" her while on the verge of happening and "ahead" of her once it has happened—behind her as future and ahead of her as past, an encompassing yet absent death. Indeed, this is the same play of anticipation and retroaction that is at work in the spectator's relation to the entire film. As we watch—as we watch the film disappear—we are suspended between two deaths: Locke's civil death in the body of another (at the beginning) and Locke's physical death in the name of another (at the end). In between, the time it takes for a man to vanish, to disappear from the world and his own self, and for the spectator to see from the viewpoint of someone who is dead, not yet but already—someone who will have been dead. If *The Adventure* had shown us "the disappearance of disappearance," *The Passenger* gives visibility to the appearance of disappearance, to disappearance itself, as a process that enmeshes the subject in a convoluted time.

What *The Passenger* stages, through a reversal of perspective, is the disappearance of the viewer herself, the fading away of the subject who sees, as she is seeing. Stretched to its extreme limits, perspective offers the seeing subject, not the imaginary object capable of filling her lack, but the *objet a*—the object of fantasy, a stopgap object, the object that "*embodies* and ultimately *images* the division of the subject, the break in the image, the cut of castration."[57] In the field of vision, Lacan leaves no doubts, this object is the gaze:[58] the gaze as it appears through anamorphosis, but also the gaze in the form of a vanishing point which, structurally and through projection, punctures the scene in more than one point. The conditions of its construction laid bare, the perspectival view is no longer a mirror in which the subject can find evidence of unity and coherence, but a mirror that reflects her own nothingness—a mirror from which she herself is excluded, a stained, shadowy mirror, with a hole as a constitutive part. As it makes visible the fading into invisibility of the subject who sees, vision expresses another kind of desire than that which seeks imaginary plenitude, a desire that binds us to death.

If there is a chalk outline, in Antonioni's films, it is not there where the corpse lies, but here where we stand as subjects of vision. In this place—a spatial and temporal position we are called to occupy by the films' formal arrangements—we come into being as the ones who disappear, as the subjects of a perception that deteriorates from within. As if vision and death were in a relation of intimacy without collapse, distance without exteriority, we see not all-at-once but in a deferred and intermittent manner; that is, we see in the mode of partial blindness. We experience the strange fecundity of being stretched to the limits, of being subjected to a vision that, because it manifests itself as deathly, comes to see what would not be otherwise visible, the very process through which it is both constituted and dismantled.

2

Desiring Death

> To the bow is given the name of life and its work is death.
>
> Heraclitus, fragment B48[1]

Intermittence

I look at the reliefs from the neo-Assyrian palaces at Nineveh that are reproduced in the British Museum catalogue—the images identified by the caption "Hunting Wild Onagers and Slaying Lions" and "King Ashurbanipal Fighting Lions on Foot and Pouring a Libation over Dead Lions." Again, I look at them as they appear in Leo Bersani's book *The Freudian Body* and, now under the spell of this admirable text on repetition, I follow the lines of force generated by a meticulous formal arrangement.[2] Spreading horizontally, without any lateral edge to counter the sense of vertical compression, the relief representing the lion hunt compels my eyes to move from left to right in a precipitous and restless manner, almost miming the frantic run of the lion and the two horses. It is only when the horseman's spear penetrates the open mouth of the other lion, the one leaping in the opposite direction, that the movement of my eyes seems to reach a sudden end. Here, in what constitutes the narrative apex of the scene and also its point of most extreme violence, my vision would thus appear to be fulfilled, at once released from the previous excitation and rendered immobile. Yet, as Bersani sharply points out, "this anecdotal climax is ambiguous."[3] My eyes continue to move—and not only forward, toward the right, carried away by the same thrust that had led them to the point of impact between the animal's mouth and the spear. They also move backward, driven by the leap of the wounded lion, and then straight toward the upper edge, along the line coinciding with the horseman's spear, nearly crossing the border of this particular scene and intruding into the one above. I now experience the irresolvable tension Bersani writes about—drawn toward the point of maximal brutality where my vision will become still, while, at the same time, disoriented by a play of forms that produces nonstop turbulence.

The relevance of such a perceptual tension can hardly be overemphasized. In the Assyrian reliefs Bersani recognizes an aesthetics that, while celebrating historical violence through the very adoption of narrativity, also persistently resists such violence by introducing a play of multiple, irreconcilable forms. Far from suggesting a state of repose, these forms are themselves endowed with the most dynamic energy—a mobile, unfocused violence, which is able to counter the destructiveness inherent in the narrative impetus, diffusing its intensity and scattering it over the entire scene. Indefatigably, this destructuration expresses a kind of "subversive passivity," a relation between the artists and the history they depict, and between the spectacle of this history and its spectator, that does not deny violence but prevents it from reaching a moment of annihilating intensity. "Catastrophe," we read next to the enlargement of the relief's climactic detail, here isolated from the larger scene, "is produced when violence stops, when the dislocations provoked by desire's mobility seek, as it were, to take place, to have a place, to become attached to particular objects and, in so doing, to destroy them."[4] Such a deadly aggressiveness would coincide with a permanently arrested perception, a state of petrification affecting the seer and the seen alike—it would end our desire to see and would deplete the visible. Here, however, relations and forms challenge the identity of even the most conventional figurative elements. In the relief representing the lion fight, Bersani notices, a curve is simultaneously an abstract line, the bar of a cage, and a section of the lion's body—and thus articulates patterns of repetition that undermine the triumph of "catastrophic violence." The offspring of a political project aimed at celebrating imperialistic power, the reliefs ultimately create a spectacle that disturbs, together with the story they ostensibly tell, the history they are meant to glorify.

I return to the relief from the lion hunt. Once more, I find myself looking at the scene of an impossible death—a catastrophe that cannot take place, that is denied a place by a subversive arrangement of forms. Caught in an excited oscillation, a back and forth movement between the lion running toward the right and the one leaping in the opposite direction, a spear piercing its mouth, I cannot see the whole scene at once nor diligently follow its unfolding from one side to the other. Instead, I perceive multiple pictures—fragments of variable extension and indistinct contour that appear in a pulsating, disorderly manner. I become the subject of a vision that is not only "agitated, erratic,"[5] but also intermittent—the subject of a strange rhythm. Emerging from the interval that separates the celebratory story line and the pure formal play—the interstice Bersani identifies but leaves unexplored—these visual fragments refuse to be ordered according to the rules of chronology and causality, and yet suggest an enduring narrative movement. They relate to each other in a convoluted manner, as if they were the flashbacks or flashforwards of a moment that does not fully exist in itself, a missing time that appears only in the almost identical repetitions it produces. As a result, the violence of the impact between the flesh and the spear is dispersed throughout the surface, returning—without ever being completely realized—in each and every one of the visual fragments I see, even those which do not directly contain its representation. Unlike catastrophic violence, this aggressiveness cannot be left behind, relegated to a time which has completely passed, nor can it be exhausted by the narrative denouement. The spectator who lets herself be carried away from the point of lethal contact is to experience, together with a heterogeneous, circular temporality, an excitement over which she has little control. Yet it is from this position of passivity—passivity toward the spectacle and its recurring violence—that she can see a picture of the past that exceeds the guidelines traced by the official discourse. A scene of victorious warfare is now a scene of murderous aggression.

As I avert my eyes from the relief, I reflect on the peculiar force that has led me back to it, not once but several times, inducing me to witness the appearance of flashlike, quasi-identical images. What kind of desire prompts a person to revisit a scene of overwhelming brutality, not to put an end to the violence there represented—not to finally reach the narrative apex which was first missed—but to maintain this violence alive, even multiply it? What kind of desire is here intertwined with my desire to see?

In *Beyond the Pleasure Principle*, Sigmund Freud discusses three cases where the compulsion to repeat an unpleasurable experience imposes itself: the dreams of patients suffering from traumatic neurosis as a consequence of life-threatening accidents or war ordeals; the play of a child staging his mother's departure and return through the aid of a wooden reel and the words *fort/da*; and finally the transference associated with the psychoanalytic cure, inducing the patient to repeat the forgotten past as if it were present, instead of remembering it as passed. Despite the complex and self-undermining character of Freud's text,[6] all these instances are normally said to show that repetition compulsion constitutes the endeavor, on the part of the subject, to retroactively master the encounter with an unforeseen traumatic event, that is, to shift from a passive to an active position in relation to a hurtful occurrence for which she was not adequately prepared.[7] Through this laborious and excruciating process, which allegedly takes place "beyond" the jurisdiction of the pleasure principle, the excitation overwhelming the subject is at last bound and the pleasure principle restored.[8] In accordance with such an argument, the return to the scene where a deadly aggression has occurred should coincide with the attempt to control its impact and eventually produce a release of tension. But, if this were the case, how could we explain our experience of Assyrian art, our attraction toward a crime scene that cannot stop returning, in the ambiguous zone between narrative and form, to the detriment of a scene which could finally be mastered?

There is, between the desire to see and the desire for death we encounter in certain works of art, a relation that exceeds the model of libidinal circulation allegedly outlined in Freud's *Beyond the Pleasure Principle*. The opposition of Eros and Thanatos, love and hate, binding and unbinding, as well as the final alignment of pleasure with discharge, domesticate the shattering force mobilized by the interpenetration of vision and death.[9] In this chapter, I will interrogate the crime scene as the configuration where the ambiguity of the death drive becomes visible, that is, where conflicting interpretations of the death drive most strongly emerge. Could we distinguish, following theorists like Bersani and Jean Laplanche,[10] between a desire for death that aims at reaching a state of immobility, a condition of inorganic stillness, and a desire that repeatedly refuses to orient itself teleologically, striving for a death which is always "already behind" and "still ahead"? Under which conditions does this other temporality of death come into view? What is at stake in conceptualizing the death drive as a principle of masochistic excitement, rather than as a principle of self-annulment and annihilation? I will address these questions while turning to Liliana Cavani's *The Night Porter*, a film that represents the compulsion to repeat as the inevitable return to the crime scene on the part of victim and aggressor alike. By retracing the film's flashbacks, I intend to show that the intermittent appearance of closely related forms generate configurations in which the present can no longer be isolated from the past and the future, thus internally fracturing the crime scene and indefinitely prolonging its duration. As a result of the rhythm of montage and the disordered temporality it produces, the spectator experiences a desire for death that, in its traumatizing impact, is productive of images which would not otherwise be visible—images relegated to oblivion when the crime scene is reduced to a single, punctual occurrence. Ultimately, I will argue, this desire for death will induce us to rethink the very desire of psychoanalysis and venture, through the notion of a creative repetition, beyond the paradigm of detection often invoked by theoreticians and practitioners alike.

The Night Porter:
The Metamorphosis of the Crime Scene

"Vienna, 1957"—time and space made specific, punctual, firmly interlocked in a caption that appears on the screen at the end of the opening titles. The Soviet troops have recently departed, and Vienna, where the bourgeoisie portrayed by painter Gustav Klimt had once lived an elegant and decadent life, is now trying to forget, to wipe out the past and begin again as if a crime against the human community had not been committed only a decade earlier.[11] The inscription is superimposed on the visual track as a man in black coat, hat, and umbrella enters the front door of the Hotel zur Oper. He is Max (Dirk Bogarde), the night porter and messenger of the guests' secret desires, and the threshold he has just crossed is the *limen* between clean, translucent, orderly streets and shadowy, labyrinthine, intensely private interiors—the chronological time of public discourse and the convoluted time of memory. It is also the *limen* between a domain in which death "takes place," realizing itself as annihilation of the other, and a sphere in which death is simultaneously "already behind" and "still ahead," prevented from occurring by a repetitive and always incomplete shattering of the self.

Their encounter in the hotel lobby is at once fortuitous and inevitable. Lucia Atherton (Charlotte Rampling) is returning from a night at the opera with her conductor husband; Max has just taken up his place behind the front desk. As they recognize each other, it is already time to part. Yet, their brief exchange of glances is indefinitely prolonged by a series of flashlike scenes, scraps of color and sound which begin to intermittently appear after they retire to their respective quarters. Directly dependent upon each character's conceptual and perceptual point of view, the flashbacks expose the time and place of their first encounter. They are in a concentration camp. Max is a Nazi officer who poses as a doctor to take sensational pictures of the prisoners; Lucia is the girl who soon becomes his favorite model. At all times, in the recollected past, the two figures are opposed according to the poles of passivity and activity—Max is filming and shooting a revolver; Lucia is being filmed and shot at. It is only the following night, when they see each other at the opera, that a disturbance is introduced into a seemingly orderly pattern. As the camera moves back and forth between them, almost miming the tension secreted by their bodies, and Lucia turns around to meet Max's piercing look, a slow process of reversal and contamination begins.

I am interested in tracing the forms through which this revolution in the field of vision and violence occurs—in documenting the perceptual transactions that enable the scopic drive and the sadomasochistic drive, here indissolubly linked, to realize their circular, loop-shaped structure. The appearance of such a structure, as Jacques Lacan emphasizes in *The Four Fundamental Concepts of Psychoanalysis*, coincides with nothing less than the constitution of the drive itself:

What is fundamental at the level of each drive is the movement outwards and back in which it is structured. It is remarkable that Freud can designate these two poles simply by using something that is the verb. *Beschauen und beschaut werden*, to see and to be seen, *quälen* and *gequält werden*, to torment and to be tormented. This is because, from the outset, Freud takes it as understood that no part of this distance covered can be separated from its outwards-and-back movement, from its fundamental reversion, from the circular character of the path of the drive.[12]

According to Lacan, the drive comes into existence insofar as the subject makes herself the object of another vision or will—seen or tormented by the other. Indeed, the subject qua subject of desire emerges exactly at this juncture, when both the departure and the end of the drive are inscribed on her own body, in a turning around that marks not self-enclosure but openness to the other. Only by exposing herself to the gaze and soliciting its effect, that is, by becoming an exhibitionist, does the voyeur assume her desire to see. Similarly, the experience of pain is accessible to the sadist only after she has transferred to the other the role she wanted for herself, that is, after she has become a masochist. "What is involved in the drive," Lacan writes, "is *making oneself seen (se faire voir)*. The activity of the drive is concentrated in this *making oneself (se faire)* . . ."[13] The reversal or return constituting the circuit of the drive involves a confusion between passivity and activity rather than a simple shifting around of positions—the drive is most active in its passive form. The vicissitudes to which Max and Lucia will submit themselves belong under the sign of this partial, impure drive.

In "Masochism and Subjectivity," Kaja Silverman argues that *The Night Porter* illustrates the extent to which passivity marks not only the female subject but also the male subject. While Lucia's victimization repeatedly coincides with her being visually exposed, the gaze that subjugates her is shown to be in excess of any actual male look. By aligning the violating gaze with the camera, the film suggests that vision originates in a site of radical alterity, that is, in an impersonal viewpoint from which Max himself is barred. Later on, when Lucia dances in front of Nazi officers at the concentration camp, we are offered an elaborate mise-en-scène displaying the autonomy of the gaze—an act of voluntary exhibitionism that disarticulates the equation of male subjectivity and scopic mastery. Indeed, Silverman claims, Max's pleasure is not the pleasure of mastery, the sadistic position being only a privileged vantage point from which the subject can enjoy a profoundly masochistic pleasure. "Max," she writes, "is fascinated not with his own cruelty, but with Lucia's pain. In fact he identifies with that pain."[14] It is in the space opened by this interpretation that I will interrogate Max and Lucia's return to a scene in which the line dividing victim and executioner is irremediably blurred—the area of radical ambiguity that Primo Levi has named the "gray zone."[15] However, as I follow their obstinate and defiant return, I will question the assumption that masochistic pleasure belongs to the present and the past as if they constituted two interconnected but ultimately distinct dimensions, focusing instead on the disrupted temporality that governs the film's affirmation of masochism. The contamination of passivity and activity which *The Night Porter* delineates is also a contamination of past, present, and future.

Subverting Forms

When Lucia decides not to follow her husband on his concert tour and remains in Vienna, fragments of memory start emerging again. She sits in the darkness of a Loos bar and a close-up of her face is interrupted by another scene—they are in the camp's hospital, Max has inflicted a wound on her arm and is now kissing it. Later, in an antique store, a pink dress captures her attention and flashes of an almost identical garment materialize—they are in the barracks, Max is slipping the dress on her seminaked body and adjusting it. Both montage sequences still gravitate around Lucia's point of view, yet the compositional pattern as well as the rhythm governing the alternation between past and present generate an identificatory process that ultimately questions the identity and self-possession of everyone at stake. I linger on the sequence and its intricate formal arrangement in the light of Bersani's suggestion: "A psychoanalytic criticism, far from seeking keys to the hidden wishes and anxieties 'behind' the text, would be the most resolutely superficial reading of texts. It would trace the continuous disappearing and reappearing of relations and forms."[16] On the right side of the screen, standing firm and fully clothed as she fondles the pink dress, Lucia assumes in the diegetic present the position which Max occupies in the recollected past. However, such a position is both intermittent and ambiguous—it only exists between past and present, in the slit opened by the pulsation of closely related visual forms. As I watch Lucia vanish there, at the right edge of the frame, where Max is appearing, and see her resurface on the left as a much younger woman, I realize that any position made available by the film represents an impossible point of anchorage for characters and spectator alike.

After Lucia secretly moves into Max's apartment, a modest residence in a peripheral Viennese neighborhood, the sequence revolving around the pink dress repeats itself through new and familiar forms. The spatial arrangement is meticulous, Lucia standing again on the right and Max occupying the portion of the screen reserved for Lucia as a girl. This time, however, identification and its vicissitudes are further complicated by the simultaneous appearance of three figures—Max, Lucia, and Lucia's specular image. Facing a full-length mirror, her back turned to the spectator, Lucia holds the dress up against her body and smiles with complicity, while Max intently observes not the static reflection but the woman in flesh and blood as she performs the part once imposed upon her. A strange temporality pervades the scene. I meet Lucia's eyes returning my look from the glaring surface of the mirror and do not know whether she is an emanation of the past or a creature of the present. The tension between temporal dimensions that had previously emerged through the rhythmic structure of montage is now inscribed in the frame's spatial configuration: Lucia is here between present and past, the double of the woman that she will have been. Then, as if to double the effect of temporal ambiguity, the scene from the camp returns, and Max is there again, on the right, wearing his Nazi uniform and slipping a pink dress on the girl who is facing him. Throughout the sequence, past and present become visible only in their mutual dependence, the past in the camp now containing traces of what will have been, the present in the apartment marked by a memory that is already other for its having been remembered. What the operation of montage—the vibration of forms between frames and within the frame—gives birth to is a time that is single and yet fragmented, fluid and yet internally punctured—a time which is repeated, interfered with, and multiplied from within. As I follow the characters trading and confusing each other's identity, I cannot locate myself in a pure and autonomous present any more than I can secure a simply active position.

That a disarticulation of well-established coordinates has occurred through character identification calls for closer attention. Among the most reliable assets of classical cinema, so-called secondary identification or identification with the characters has been under attack for rendering the cinematic apparatus invisible and promoting the spectator's insertion into normative gender, class, and race positions.[17] According to Stephen Heath, the alignment between spectator and character realizes the conversion of the screen's "space" into a narrative "place," thus reaffirming a perspectival arrangement that maintains the subject in a centered and immobile position, imprisoned by a desire for imaginary plenitude.[18] Feminist theorists like Ann Friedberg and Mary Ann Doane also denounce the ideologically pernicious influence of secondary identification, namely, its capacity to reduce difference and assimilate otherness in support of the existing power structure.[19] However, in her work on political cinema, Kaja Silverman argues that identification does not inherently and automatically serve the dominant order—that, on the contrary, it is endowed with a unique potential for subversion.[20] Because the imaginary register is constitutive of our subjectivity not once and for all but over and over, throughout infantile as well as adult life, identification represents not only an irreducible operation but also a privileged vehicle for psychic and social transformation. I will turn to her work, as it promises to shed light on the complex scenario we encountered in *The Night Porter*, where identification functions not at the service of cinematic suture but on behalf of the cut or wound which is exposed, exploring its texture and redefining its contours.[21]

Drawing on the French psychoanalyst Henri Wallon and the German philosopher Max Scheler, as well as on several early film theorists, Silverman proposes to conceptualize cinematic identification as potentially excorporative or "heteropathic," rather than unavoidably incorporative or "idiopathic."[22] The distinction is of the outmost importance. If idiopathic variety is predicated upon the ego's thirst for sameness and unity—a thirst which only the murderous assimilation of another self can temporarily satisfy—heteropathic variety preserves an unbridgeable distance between the subject and the other, allowing a process of seduction into difference to take place. The spectator who identifies according to an exteriorizing logic abandons her own corporeal coordinates—her sensational ego and the specular image to which she is bound by a proprietary relationship—and adventurously goes exploring the other's bodily framework.[23] A passage from Béla Balázs's *Theory of the Film* further elucidates the kind of "transport or abduction" which cinematic identification is capable of realizing:

In the cinema the camera carries the spectator into the film picture itself. . . . Although we sit in our seats . . . we do not see Romeo and Juliet from there. We look up to Juliet's balcony with Romeo's eyes and look down on Romeo with Juliet's. Our eye and with it our consciousness is identified with the characters in the film, we look at the world out of their eyes and have no angle of vision of our own. We walk amid crowds, ride, fly or fall with the hero and if one character looks into the other's eyes, he looks into our eyes from the screen, for, our eyes are in the camera and become identical with the gaze of the characters. They see with our eyes.[24]

While occupying a confined place in the movie theater, the spectator who watches a filmed version of Shakespeare's *Romeo and Juliet* is transported into the picture through a creative use of cinematic technology—the changing distance between spectator and scene, the division of a scene into shots, the variation of angle, perspective, and focus, the close-up, and montage.[25] In a self-expropriating move, she leaves her own look behind and adopts the characters' perspective, shifting from one character to the other even when this entails, as Silverman points out, a traversal of gender lines.[26]

The extent to which the identificatory process can entail a disruption of the self's integrity is illustrated by a fable, which Scheler employs as an allegory about heteropathy and idiopathy and Silverman discusses to underscore the primacy of the corporeal dimension:

A white squirrel, having met the gaze of a snake, hanging on a tree and showing every sign of a mighty appetite for its prey, is so petrified by this that it gradually moves towards instead of away from the snake, and finally throws itself into the open jaws. . . . Plainly the squirrel's instinct for self-preservation has succumbed to an ecstatic participation in the object of the snake's own appetitive nisus, namely "swallowing." The squirrel identifies in feeling with the snake, and thereupon spontaneously establishes corporeal identity with it, by disappearing down its throat.[27]

As Silverman points out, the white squirrel perceives and behaves according to an excorporative model. She is the heteropath who relinquishes her own bodily boundaries, submitting herself to the shape of another. The snake, on the contrary, approaches difference with an indomitable appetite for incorporation, a desire that finds literal expression in the dynamics of ingestion. She is the idiopath who, all the incongruent elements having been absorbed, can finally reaffirm an autonomous and coherent identity.

Through a multifaceted use of montage, *The Night Porter* not only performs but also foregrounds the process of abduction described above—it puts heteropathic identification on display, presenting us with characters that are themselves repeatedly engaged in ecstatic perceptual transactions. As a result, the bodily ego the spectator comes to assume, whether it is Max's or Lucia's, is not an individual, discrete entity but a constellation or assemblage of heterogeneous traits—gestures and affects that take shape in between different characters. By virtue of its dazzling montage, the film also rewrites Scheler's story—a story that dramatizes, together with the procedures of identification, the relentless work of the death drive, exposing its masochistic as well as its sadistic components. The squirrel can identify heteropathically because her "instinct for self-preservation" has yielded to a desire for "ecstatic participation" that coincides with the radical unbinding or deforming of her own bodily coordinates, while the snake identifies idiopathically by letting aggressiveness fulfill itself through the dissolution of the other's bodily envelope.[28] Yet, our analysis has shown, Max and Lucia could not be symmetrically aligned with the allegorical figures of squirrel and snake, at least not in any static and inflexible manner. Not only do they rhythmically exchange positions, taking turns in assuming the roles of predator and prey. They also perform the same primordial scene repeatedly and incompletely, always stopping before the end, interrupting their reciprocal and deadly attraction before the climax is reached. In the story, whether the emphasis falls on the squirrel's unconditional surrender or on the snake's triumphant attack, the death drive operates as a principle of discharge and annihilation—it forces death to realize itself in the present, to take place as catastrophe. In the film, where Max and Lucia create a play of forms without narrative resolution—a performance unfulfilled by death—the death drive functions as a principle of masochistic excitement, inducing desire not to expire but to circulate between the anticipation and the postponement of death.[29] The time of the death drive is here a time out of joint, in which death will have always taken place—a circular time that offers no escape but also no instantaneous release. The implications are far-reaching. Since "the drive, the partial drive," Lacan reminds us, "is profoundly a death drive,"[30] such a convoluted time is also what marks the very emergence of the subject, in the looping around, the always missed coincidence between seeing and being seen, tormenting and being tormented.

One sequence above all enacts the suspended play I have just sketched. Wearing Max's sweater, a slip, and a child's shoes which are too small for her—once more, a figure showing the traces of multiple identities—Lucia abruptly runs to the bathroom and locks the door. Inside, the camera registers a moment of hesitation, then her deliberate gestures. She seizes a bottle of perfume and shatters it on the floor, right in front of the door, turns the key and swiftly steps back. Max, who has been pounding on the door trying to force his way in, all of a sudden encounters no resistance and finds himself stepping on the broken glass—he smiles in response, taking visible pleasure in the pain he is experiencing. Then, as he lightly lifts his wounded foot, Lucia slides her hand underneath. They stare at each other, and Max steps down on it, causing the glass fragments to penetrate deeper into his own flesh, while simultaneously piercing her fingers and palm. Now it is Lucia's turn; she smiles with the same intensity. During this prolonged and fragile exchange masochistic enjoyment seizes both of them, not at the same time but at intervals too short to be detected. Because they move back and forth between activity and passivity, never occupying any permanent single position, each one of them can identify excorporatively without being incorporated and destroyed by the other. Here, the identificatory process undergone by the snake and the squirrel remains incomplete, coming to coincide with the assumption of the other's shape in a time which is not the present—producing not the dissolution of one bodily ego for the sake of another but a reciprocal subversion of forms. After the film's last flashback shows Lucia delicately kissing Max's chest, we are given yet another interlacing of hands and feet, as the two lovers wash the blood off each other's wounds. We have now fully entered a domain in which the death drive could be dissociated from unfulfilled masochistic excitement only at the expense of life itself.[31] It is not by sheer coincidence that the sequence closes with Max's realization that they are under surveillance and will soon be under siege.

Erasing Forms

As she wanders through the hotel's underground corridors, during the time that precedes her decision to move into Max's apartment, Lucia becomes the spectator of a most peculiar reunion. Gathered around a large table are Max and his friends, all former Nazis, intently discussing the preliminaries of an upcoming hearing. The group comprises Hans Vogler (Gabriele Ferzetti), who is addressed as "professor" and displays psychoanalytic expertise; Klaus (Philippe Leroy), who claims authority on investigative and legal matters, having access to the government's files on war criminals; a homosexual dancer (Amedeo Amodio) who used to perform for them in the camp; and two alleged businessmen. In a severe parody of the Law and the Freudian cure, what they are planning is alternatively referred to as "trial" or "group analysis," the end and the means being considered the same—the removal of guilt through meticulous confession. All members of the group have already endured this process, gaining, as a result, a sense of liberation from the past, together with the entitlement to resume honorable professions. All except Max: the last one on the list, he is accused of living "as a church mouse," having chosen to do an obscure job in a society that strives to rebuild its lost glory. In front of his peers, Max criticizes the process's therapeutic effectiveness as well as its morality, and shows signs of resistance in submitting to it, especially now that a witness for the prosecution has come back from the dead. He has yet to inform the others about such an unexpected return, fearing not his conviction but the witness's demise. He knows very well that, under the group's rules, every defendant is eventually acquitted but that, for him to remain innocent, the evidence which has been painstakingly collected has to be destroyed or, in Klaus's words, "filed away." That is, papers and photographs are to be burned and living witnesses assassinated. We observe the scene from Lucia's viewpoint, as she stands behind the door that is ajar, in a zone of imperfect darkness. When she runs away, glimpses of her perturbed demeanor are intercut with Max's expressions.

In her article on *The Night Porter*, Silverman underscores that the group, as a whole, is firmly positioned on the side of the ego, performing the inhibitive and defensive functions proper to it. According to the rules of the secondary process, the group uses language to bind the unpleasurable affect generated through recollection and increase its own cohesiveness. Max and Lucia, on the other hand, allow their perceptions and actions to occur under the dominance of the primary process, refusing to bind or "translate" the exciting pain of recollection into a culturally enforced, stable, and homogeneous representation of life. The distinction is crucial to my argument on temporality and the death drive. When death is envisioned according to a model of catastrophic violence, as an event which realizes itself in the present, the death drive is not opposed but ultimately conducive to the binding and consolidating of the ego. In the case of the group, desiring death becomes the ultimate expression of narcissism, not the condition of its diffusion—it sanctions the imaginary coherence Lacan attributes to the ego, at the expense of the subject's relation to the signifier.[32] The danger posed by Max and Lucia coincides here with the introduction of another temporality—theirs is a desire for death in the future anterior, a shattering force that radically undermines any aspiration to the mastery and destruction of the other. Significantly, these two conflicting interpretations of the death drive shape the way in which memory is conceived and practiced at the personal as well as collective level. The group, while pursuing death as annihilation, is set to implement an erasure of forms—to methodically produce oblivion as "that which effaces . . . the signifier as such."[33] Max and Lucia, on the contrary, submit themselves to masochistic transactions that repeatedly avoid death—the attainment of death, its taking place—thus preserving the play of signifiers from dissolution. In its strange and threatening fecundity, their fascination with a death out of joint engenders the possibility, not merely to remember, but to remember along lines that are not traced beforehand.

Despite the pressure exercised by the group, Max will not give up Lucia. For him, what is at stake is neither confession nor the assumption of guilt. If he works at night, hiding like a church mouse, it is because he experiences "a sense of shame in the light"—shame, not guilt, is the affect which marks his being. Similarly, Lucia will not seek refuge

in the authorities investigating her disappearance. She continues to remain with Max "of [her] own free will," even when the professor and his
friends put them under armed surveillance, severing all communications
between the apartment in which they hide and the outside world—until,
one night, exhausted by confinement and lack of food, they prepare for
their last performance. They leave the apartment—Max in full Nazi uniform, Lucia in pink dress and white shoes—and drive away, knowing
they will be followed. At dawn, they stop on a majestic modern bridge.
While walking toward the scene's vanishing point, they are executed in
unhurried succession. Their bodies occupy the screen for a few moments,
then the film ends. The fulfillment of the group's desire for catastrophic
violence, this last scene is left to mark the coincidence between narrative climax and eclipse—the evacuation of exciting pain and the final
disappearance of forms. If the crime scene returning in Max and Lucia's
masochistic play is radically split, multiplied, spread over time—the
past becoming the effect of the moment it produces, the future which it
will have been—the crime scene willed by the group has precise spatial
and temporal boundaries. It can be examined, solved, and eventually
archived or filed away. Against the heterogeneous, creative memory affirmed by the couple's desire for death in the future anterior—a desire
that has thoroughly permeated the film's enunciative strategies—the denouement imposed by the group coincides with nothing less than the
effacement of vision. That such a configuration of death and oblivion is
here aligned with the figures of the analyst and the investigator deserves
special consideration—after all, since the end of the nineteenth century,
psychoanalysis and criminal investigation have asserted themselves as
prominent models for reconstructing the past.

The Detective and the Witness

As the siege is about to begin, the professor intrudes into Max's
apartment and speaks to Lucia. She is there alone, restrained by a long
chain which Max has fastened to her wrist, fearing the group might take
her away. Faced with Lucia's obstinacy, the professor says that he cannot force her to "remember"—he is there only to ask her to "testify."
Only after the trial will Max and his friends be able to live "in peace,"

as respected citizens, the symptoms as well as the causes of their neurosis having been removed. His careful use of words, together with the fact that following her testimony Lucia cannot but become an inconvenient witness, to be disposed of, points to a friction in the domain of memory—a crisis marking the formal procedures meant to foster and safeguard it. A profoundly psychoanalytic film, *The Night Porter* induces us to question the relation between psychoanalysis, detection, and testimony, foregrounding the dangers inherent in a conception of time that ultimately separates the future from the past. I believe that, though here associated with formal procedures meant to domesticate memory, psychoanalysis can help us envision the time of testimony as the time of creative repetition—what we might call, after Lacan and the notion of full speech discussed in Chapter 4, remembrance in the future anterior. Such a reconfiguration of testimony, however, becomes available only after psychoanalysis itself critically engages its own relationship to the trial and the model of juridical witnessing to which all witnessing is often assimilated.

In their work on the radical crisis of witnessing generated by the Holocaust, which is there defined as an "event without a witness," "an event eliminating its own witness," Shoshana Felman and Dori Laub elaborate a theory of testimony that relies on the juridical notions of responsibility, truth, and evidence. At the beginning of the chapter devoted to Claude Lanzmann's film *Shoah* (1985), Felman firmly positions the witness within the symbolic space of the courtroom:

To bear witness is to take responsibility for truth: to speak, implicitly, from within the legal pledge and the juridical imperative of the witness's oath. . . . To testify is always, metaphorically, to take the witness stand . . . thus not merely to narrate but to commit oneself, and to commit the narrative, to others . . . [in order] to enable a decision by a judge or jury—metaphorical or literal—about the true nature of the facts of an occurrence; to enable an objective reconstruction of what history was like, irrespective of the witness.[34]

Whether before a court of law or before the court of civilization, the witness is called to speak the truth as that which is given in advance, objectively and independently of her statement. Facing the contradiction which, at this point, emerges between the impersonal character she has just attributed to testimony and the unique, irreplaceable role each and every witness is acknowledged to perform—"If someone else could have written my stories," writes Elie Wiesel, "I would not have written them"[35]—Felman appeals to the legal and epistemological tradition of the Western world, where witnessing is essentially defined in relation to firsthand seeing. Because she has seen with her own eyes—because she has been the subject of a direct, unmediated vision—the witness speaks in conformity with the law of evidence, and her speech can be used to determine "what really happened," to expose the past "the way it really was."[36]

According to this model of testimony, the historian and the filmmaker who, in *Shoah*, appear next to the eyewitnesses are considered as "second-degree witnesses," "witnesses of witnesses." Within the film, as well as in the relation between the film and its audience, they play a vital role, performing what Felman calls "the task of the translator,"[37] that of deciphering and rendering intelligible unfamiliar signs—a task which, throughout the book, she also assigns to the psychoanalyst. If the patient, the one who has survived a trauma, occupies the position of witness, the analyst enters the therapeutic relation as the other witness, the witness to the witness that the survivor struggles to be. "The doctor's testimony," Felman specifies, "does not substitute itself for the patient's testimony, but *resonates with it*, because, as Freud discovers, *it takes two to witness the unconscious*."[38] It is only within the psychic space engendered by this double witnessing that the truth of the unconscious can emerge. Speech is the event that enables the truth to realize, not to constitute, itself, the truth preceding and exceeding any statement of which the witness is capable.

Felman's conception of psychoanalysis as testimony—as the form of testimony that recognizes the unintended, unintentional contribution of those who are called to bear witness—would thus seem to counterbalance the model through which psychoanalytic work has often been understood. I refer here to the epistemological paradigm that, according to Carlo Ginzburg, "quietly emerged in the sphere of the social sciences" toward the end of the nineteenth century.[39] Based on conjectural reasoning, on the careful interpretation of "signs and scraps of evidence," this model draws together three pivotal figures of the modern world—the art historian, the detective, and the analyst—thus establishing an isomorphic relation between features of painting, clues, and symptoms, that is, between the space of the representation, the crime scene, and the dream. In the field of art history, the so-called "Morelli method" allowed scholars to distinguish almost perfect copies from the unique original on account of minor details—fingernails, earlobes, halos—details which would normally escape notice, being positioned below the threshold of ordinary perception. It is through marginal details that the artist "gives himself away," as does the criminal when he unwillingly leaves a fingerprint at the murder scene, and the patient when he reveals the apparently insignificant detail of a dream. In "The Moses of Michelangelo," Freud himself points out the remarkable similarities between psychoanalysis and the investigative procedure developed by Morelli. "It seems to me," he writes, "that his method of inquiry is closely related to the technique of psychoanalysis. It, too, is accustomed to divine secret and concealed things from despised or unnoticed figures, from the rubbish-heap, as it were, of our observation."[40]

As far as testimony is understood in juridical terms, the analogy between the analyst and the witness proposed by Felman still partakes of the epistemological model I have outlined. Both the investigation and the trial look at the crime scene as the index or trace of an event that, while having irrupted into the present and threatened the future, ultimately belongs to the past, and to the past only—past, present, and future being posited as independent and consecutive temporal dimensions.[41] In this respect, Felman consistently speaks of history in the past tense, and Ginzburg leaves no doubt—the work of interpretation coincides with the development of a narrative oriented toward the past, a story aimed at the reconstruction of what happened before and after a deed is carried out. While distinguishing between "the Sherlock Holmes way" and "the Philip Marlowe way,"[42] the classical detective and the hard-boiled sleuth, Slavoj Žižek also identifies detection, as well as its analytic counterpart, with the articulation of a narrative that is finally able to restore chronological time, so that the past can come to light the way it really was. "The detective novel," he writes, "is the story of the detective's effort to tell the story, to reconstruct what "really happened" around and before the murder: the novel is finished when the detective is finally able to tell 'the real story' in the form of a linear narrative."[43] When a traumatic event occurs, the natural succession of past, present, and future is disturbed or shattered, and what Žižek calls "the unnarrated" emerges as that which resists symbolization. It is part of the investigator's task to transform this residue into an intelligible story, thus reinstating the temporal progression which the trauma had disrupted.

I am suspicious of this kind of temporality and the political implications it tends to hide. I look back at the struggle over memory that, in *The Night Porter*, opposes the group to Max and Lucia. I also recall Walter Benjamin's distinction between the homogeneous, continuous, empty time marking official historiography and the heterogeneous, discontinuous, filled time engendered by those who "stop telling the sequence of events like the beads of a rosary"[44]—the materialist historian, the heretical storyteller. I will then ask: how can psychoanalysis help us articulate forms of time that radically defy any clear-cut distinction between past, present, and future, even beyond the logic of deferred action or "afterwardsness"?[45] How can we say, "the past is never dead, it has not even passed,"[46] without remaining confined to the compulsive repetition of the same? I turn once more to testimony and wonder if a nonjuridical notion of witnessing could lead to the emergence of a memory that secretes, together with different stories, another way of writing history.

In his work on Auschwitz, Giorgio Agamben compellingly argues against the confusion of ethical and juridical categories, and the consequent understanding of truth and justice in terms of judgment. Confronted by the zone where the line dividing victim and executioner is irremediably blurred, where the oppressed becomes the oppressor and the oppressor is in turn oppressed—the area of irresponsibility that Primo Levi has named the "gray zone"—the law cannot exhaust the question of witnessing. Indeed, the law itself is called into question by the constitution of such a zone, to the extent that witnessing can only take place where the law is not. In Agamben's words: "A non-juridical element of truth exists such that the *quaestio facti* can never be reduced to the *quaestio iuris*. This is precisely what concerns the survivor: everything that places a human action beyond the law, radically withdrawing it from the

Trial."[47] The survivor is a *superstes*, that is, a person who has lived through a traumatic event and can therefore speak about it as a witness—as such, she cannot be also a *testis*, that is, a third party in a trial or lawsuit between two opponents, a neutral witness. Her testimony exists outside the domain of the trial, in isolation from the collection and evaluation of evidence distinguishing all legal procedure.

Yet, as Primo Levi repeatedly claims, the survivor is not the true witness. Because she has survived, she has also, to some extent, enjoyed a privilege—she is not the rule but the exception. She has not experienced the destiny of the common prisoner, the *Muselmann*, the "mummyman," the one who had entered that irreversible state of living death that was systematically produced in the camp.[48] Only the Muslim, the one who has drowned, would be the complete witness. But the common prisoner—the one whose testimony would have a general relevance—cannot speak, and could not have spoken even when she was still "alive," because her death had begun long before the termination of her vital functions. Months before her final demise, she had lost the ability to think, observe, remember, speak in an intelligible manner. Far from being an "eyewitness," the true witness is thus the one who could not see—"she who has seen the Gorgon,"[49] writes Levi, that is, she who has seen "the anti-face, the impossibility of seeing."[50] The survivor speaks on her behalf—or, as Levi says, "by proxy"[51]—and can thus be considered a witness in the sense expressed by the Latin term *auctor*, "author." In the classical world, Agamben reminds us, every author was always conceived as a coauthor, never creating ex nihilo but in all cases building on something which already existed. As *auctor*-witness, the survivor relies on something else, something other—word, image, event—which precedes her and, not being complete in itself, needs her intervention in order to grow. "The survivor and the *Muselmann*, the tutor and the incapable person, and the creator and his material," writes Agamben, "are inseparable; their unity-difference alone constitutes testimony."[52] Testimony stems from the essential noncoincidence between the survivor and the true witness, the one who can speak and the silent being. Unlike the archive and the Babelic library, ready to reveal their secrets under the solicitation of the historian's inquisitive eye, testimony inhabits the in-between separating language as potentiality from the impossibility of speech.

It is only as "author"—as creator of a language that at once implicates and exceeds her—that the survivor can bear witness to the dead. Immersed in the dark region of silence, her gesture is akin to that of the poet, the "author" par excellence, the one who speaks the impossibility of speaking. Could we envision analysis as another zone of experimentation, a mode of creation other than poetry but in a relation of intimacy with it, in which testimony—the lacuna inherent in all testimony—can be conceived and performed as that which is in excess of any juridical paradigm? Could we think of the analyst as yet another coauthor, a strange creator who, together with the survivor, bears witness to a past that is not dead, that indeed has not even passed—a time which, because it belongs to the dead, will always be a concern of the future?

I believe the time of analysis as nonjuridical testimony would in this case coincide with a circular time—the chiasm of past and future, the intertwining of dimensions that are never autonomous and yet always distinct. The past was not once and for all. Instead, it cannot stop having been and returns in the future as it has been transformed by the future itself. Indeed, this convoluted temporality could constitute a form of witnessing in itself, independent of the content, being the affirmation of that movement of anticipation and retroaction which characterizes the future anterior as the time of our existence. Such a possibility acquires a particular relevance if we dwell, together with Levi and Agamben, on the condition of the *Muselmänner*, the living dead, those whose death could no longer be called death, because they did not die but were fabricated as corpses or, rather, figures, dolls, rags.[53] Where death is present every day, everywhere, anonymous as a bureaucratic affair, where the thought of death is incessantly materialized, the very possibility of authentic temporality—what Heidegger calls "Being-towards-death"—is radically undermined. In the camp, past and future, anticipation and having been are flattened onto each other—dying simply means "being liquidated." To affirm a temporality in which the chiasmatic relation between past and future is once again viable—to reaffirm this temporality not in a spirit of triumph but against the abyss opened by the conflation of death and mere decease—could then constitute in itself a form of testimony.

If I now return, at the end of this questioning of psychoanalysis as detection, to Liliana Cavani's *The Night Porter*, it is not to determine whether Max is Lucia's other witness, or whether their relationship irremediably challenges the very possibility of psychoanalysis as a regimented therapeutic practice. (Although the temptation is to underscore the dangers of a model that, like in the case of the group, subordinates the turmoil of remembrance to healing and proper social functioning.) Rather, it is to say explicitly what I have thus far only suggested: that the film itself constitutes a novel act of testimony (and not only because it gives visibility to Lucia's shattering memories, not even in view of the distinction it draws, at the diegetic level, between the chronological order enforced by the group and the intricate temporality created by the couple's sadomasochistic play). Through multiple formal devices—most notably, the rhythmic structure of montage—*The Night Porter* affirms the temporality of the future anterior in its relationship to the spectator. As I follow the film's elegant and restless forms, I too experience the possibility to remember a memory that comes from the future. I too become the dispersed subject of a creative repetition, the witness to a subversive act of testimony.

3

Seeing Time

For the weight of the natural world is already a weight
of the past. Each landscape of my life, because it is
not a wandering troop of sensations or a system of
ephemeral judgments but a segment of the durable
flesh of the world, is qua visible, pregnant with many
other visions besides my own, and the visible that I see,
of which I speak, even if it is not Mount Hymettus or the
plane trees of Delphi, is numerically the same that Plato
and Aristotle saw and spoke of.

Maurice Merleau-Ponty[1]

Skins of Color

Mount Sainte-Victoire, 1888–90; *Mount Sainte-Victoire, Seen from Bibemus*, ca. 1897; *Mount Sainte-Victoire, Seen from Les Lauves*, 1902–4; *Mount Sainte-Victoire, Seen from Les Lauves*, 1904–6; *Mount Sainte-Victoire, Seen from Les Lauves*, 1905. Five among the thirty oils and forty-five watercolors of the massif Cézanne painted throughout the years, approaching the mountain from diverse angles, at varying times of the day, in different seasons; five color plates from a monograph, which are now lying on the desk next to me. They solicit my attention with meticulous intensity, exercising a power of attraction that persists despite the changes in texture, color, and luminosity brought about by mechanical reproduction. Silently they induce my body to move, my eyes to turn and linger on a surface that I know not to be smooth, even if I cannot touch it, because I have seen the Baltimore and Philadelphia pictures in flesh and blood, and can still feel the unevenness they imprinted on my eyes. There, in those unique patches, are the traces of innumerable brushstrokes—sedimented layers of paint and time. "It took him one hundred working sessions for a still life, one hundred fifty sittings for a portrait,"[2] writes Maurice Merleau-Ponty in his inaugural essay on the philosophy of painting. Dab after dab, starting with the dark areas, he would shape the object through the overlapping of multiple color tones—reds, yellows, blues, greens, and black. He would also leave blank, unfinished areas.[3] Now this surface on which the laborious process of translation between artist and landscape has been inscribed draws my body increasingly closer to itself and, while making impossible any full contact, begins to disclose the strata of a mysterious depth. The awareness that Cézanne "was seeking depth all his life" only intensifies the strangeness of an encounter I have only begun to live through.[4]

Merleau-Ponty devotes important pages to the question of depth. In "Cézanne's Doubt," he distinguishes between the lived perspective, which emerges with our acts of perception, and the artificial perspective, which is imposed upon us by traditional painting and photography. If Cézanne studies the latter, geometry being among his central preoccupations, it is only to achieve the former, that is, "to depict matter as it takes on form, the birth of order through spontaneous organization."[5] The result never ceases to surprise us—space is at once crystalline and fluid, tightly structured and vibrant. Cézanne's idiosyncratic working procedure testifies to the complex nature of his canvasses. "To paint a landscape properly I first have to know the geological strata," he said to Joachim Gasquet, the young poet who used to join his daily wanderings through the countryside of Provence. Later, he would look at the landscape wide-eyed, and cover his initial sketch of the geological layering with flecks of color, according to the modulation method described above. "Nature is not an affair of the surface; it is in depth. Colors express that depth on the surface." By dissolving the partition between outline and colors, Cézanne allows the pictorial surface to show the depth of the natural world at its fullest. It is the creation of a new mode in painting and, at the same time, the rediscovery of a dimension preceding any distinction between the senses—a primordial, prescientific world in which vision and touch cannot be set apart. Here, Merleau-Ponty reminds us, "we *see* the depth, the smoothness, the softness, the hardness of objects; Cézanne even claimed that we see their odor."[6] Color does not conjure up depth from outside, by evoking tactile sensations—it is of touch as depth is of vision.

In "Eye and Mind," Merleau-Ponty further develops his interrogation of depth and the aesthetic experience. Painters like Cézanne, Matisse, and Klee show us that depth is not a third dimension drawn from the other two, the result of a geometric procedure that treats space as homogeneous and in itself, that is, beyond each and every point of view. "Something about space evades our attempts to survey it from above,"[7] he explains, at once challenging Descartes' *Dioptrics* and the theoreticians of Renaissance perspective. Space is not a system of relations between objects, extended matter which can be viewed impartially or assessed from outside. On the contrary, it must be conceived in relation to the lived body—the body I experience while inhabiting the world, not trying to manipulate it, the body the painter knows to be immersed in the visible and not positioned in front of it. Only with respect to such an understanding of space can we begin to appreciate what several painters have described—the feeling of being looked at by the things they had set out to observe. Far from producing a tear in the realm of perception, the painter's experience brings us back to the paradoxical reflexivity of the sensible, that reversibility between the seer and the seen, the toucher and the touched, that our body remarkably exemplifies:

The enigma derives from the fact that my body simultaneously sees and is seen. That which looks at all things can also look at itself and recognize, in what it sees, the "other side" of its power of looking. It sees itself seeing; it touches itself touching; it is visible and sensitive for itself. It is a self, not by transparency, like thought, which never thinks anything except by assimilating it, constituting it, transforming it into thought—but a self by confusion, narcissism, inherence of the see-er in the seen, the toucher in the touched, the feeler in the felt—a self then, that is caught up in things, having a front and a back, a past and a future.[8]

In the same way the body can touch only because it is touched in return, the body can see only because it is also visible, enmeshed in the fabric of the world. There is, between our carnal being and things, an interpenetration that defies all classical dichotomies—the body and the world, Merleau-Ponty emphasizes, are made of the same "stuff."[9] Perception occurs in this zone beyond the autonomous self, where activity and passivity can hardly be differentiated and it becomes impossible to ascertain who sees and what is seen.

Cézanne's paintings of Mount Sainte-Victoire revive the perceptual confusion that is at the heart of our existence. As my eyes pause on their surface, I see Cézanne seeing the mountain and the mountain seeing him—the painter becoming what is painted and the painted expressing itself through him who paints, in a reciprocal exchange of forms.[10] Until I too find myself emerging from the depth of the landscape, engulfed by the foliage, the meadows, the rocks, and those darker patches that in the Zurich picture blend with the green used to mark the atmospheric fluctuations. It slowly becomes palpable that Mount Sainte-Victoire is far more than a sum of geophysical features—that, in its very materiality, it is already a constellation of memories and expectations, a configuration superseding the spatial domain. We know that at fifty-one Cézanne retreated to Aix-en-Provence, "where he found landscape best suited to his genius but where also he returned to the world of his childhood, his mother and sister."[11] There, at over a thousand meters, Mount Sainte-Victoire stands out not only for its size but also for the weight of its history. Once the site of cultic rituals, the mountain has witnessed the fierce battles between general Marius and the tribe of the Cimbri in 102 B.C., the arrival of Christian hermits in the fifth century, the construction of a Camaldolite monastery twelve hundred years later. In Cézanne's time, pilgrimages and midsummer celebrations still took place amid its scenery, and it is certain that the young painter and his friends explored it again and again, during wanderings and overnight excursions. Only a few years before he died, Cézanne left his town apartment and moved into a studio house from which he could enjoy a full view of the mountain. By then Mount Sainte-Victoire had become the dominant motif, the majestic center of his paintings.

The depth of the visible which is around me exceeds not only the gridlike space of geometry, with its absolute lines and discrete points, but also the time of the now. Rather than existing in a self-enclosed and autonomous present, such depth is caught up in a multiplicity of temporal dimensions. Yet it would be faulty to think that the landscape I see merely points to a past and a future—that it recalls or anticipates the past and the future as if they were external to it and could be arranged, in some abstract domain, according to the order of chronology. This depth I inhabit but cannot possess is other than the indirect trace of what once was or someday will be. The skins of color Cézanne lays on his canvasses do not evoke the days of the Roman invasion or the nights when festive bonfires were lit any more than they simply "suggest" tactile sensations. There is, between the visible and time, an intimacy that challenges the traditional separation of subject and object, activity and passivity, inside and outside. In this chapter, I will explore the idea that "time offers itself to him who wishes only to 'see it,'" which Merleau-Ponty had begun to elaborate in *The Visible and the Invisible*. What does it mean to see, rather than represent or measure, time? Since the visible is endowed with an inexhaustible depth, can we also think time as deep? Can we conceive it as holding different degrees or levels of depth? Is there a reversibility of time, a winding of past and present, in the same way in which there is a reversibility of perception, an intertwining of seeing and being seen?

I will address these questions as they take shape at the crossroads of film and philosophy, following the enigmatic, circular thread of Pier Paolo Pasolini's *Oedipus Rex*. By focusing on the shots marking the encounter between the protagonist and the meadow of his infancy, I will show that the same landscape, qua fragment of the visible, presents us with the coexistence of multiple temporal layers. However, it will become apparent that, far from belonging to anyone as individual property, the depth of the visible constitutes a memory in excess of our subjectivity, indeed the memory through which our own subjectivity is defined—a visual intertwining of past and present that, being anonymous or impersonal, engenders singular and yet not autonomous acts of perception. It will also become apparent that, with respect to this depth, Pasolini's cinema of poetry constitutes a site of both perceptual emergence and philosophical articulation—not the site where an externally formed thought exercises itself but the very site where vision directly thinks its own enigma, without attempting to solve it or translate it according to a model-in-thought.[12]

Oedipus Rex: The Depth of the Crime Scene

In "A Philosophical View of the Detective Novel," Ernst Bloch identifies the detective genre's fundamental characteristics—the suspense connected with the process of guessing; the conjectural activity which, through a careful evaluation of clues, leads to the act of discovery; and, most importantly, the omission of the pivotal event: the detective story opens on a crime which has already been committed. It is this very omission, Bloch emphasizes, which provides the genre with its specific narrative form, namely, "the form of a picture puzzle."[13] However, in most cases, the scene of the crime that faces detective and reader alike does not immediately appear as a picture puzzle but presents a natural, almost organic wholeness. Slavoj Žižek points out that such unity constitutes the first mark of deception—the result of the murderer's attempt to cover up the dreadful act. The detective's inaugural challenge is to recognize that something is wrong or missing, thereby denaturalizing the scene and transforming it into "a bricolage of heterogeneous elements."[14] The term *clue* indicates the very detail that allows the process of estrangement to occur and the search for the missing pieces to begin. Often unobtrusive and trivial to the untrained eye, it calls the detective's attention by virtue of its structural position. The analogy between the detective and the psychoanalyst becomes most significant precisely at this juncture. If the dream, as Freud states, can read like a rebus or picture puzzle, it is because the interpreter is able to breach its apparent consistency, a quality which is nothing but the product of secondary revision. As far as one looks for the so-called symbolic meaning, that is, the hidden meaning of the dream's pictorial elements, the latent dream-thought will never emerge. Only by identifying the detail that stands in for what has been repressed, expunged from the manifest dream-content, does the process of interpretation begin.[15]

Simultaneously a return to the most exemplary detective story and to the formative myth of psychoanalysis, Pasolini's *Oedipus Rex* destabilizes the set of formal procedures I have briefly described. At the level of both diegesis and enunciation it defies the investigative impetus that transforms a portion of the visible into a picture puzzle, affirming a cinematic style devoted to the interrogation, not manipulation, of perception. There, where the detective sees the traces of an event which has already occurred, a scene that needs to be deconstructed and then rearranged in relation to homogeneous space and chronological time, Pasolini and his new Oedipus will see a depth they cannot master—a depth that, we will discover, is at once of the visible and of time. That such a vision entails the subject's radical decentering, his dispersion through the multiple layers of what does not belong to him, is most clearly manifested in the encounter between the human face and the landscape. I will privilege two sequences above all others—carefully positioned at the beginning and at the end of the film, they constitute each other's imperfect double, immersing character and spectator alike into a depth that cannot be contained within the spatial and temporal parameters of any individual existence.

Experimenting with Free Indirect Subjectivity

"Thebes"—carved on a large stone, above a stylized hand pointing to the right, the word appears in the film's opening shot. It is there, immovable and discreet, not to mark the time and place of the Greek myth, but to inaugurate a detour through modern life. What follows is a series of tableaux—a village in the distance, a modest square, a two-story house in which a baby is born. Later, in the meadow, the baby is lying on the grass, while several young women are chasing each other and laughing. Repeatedly, liberating its visionary potential, the camera assumes the viewpoint of the infant and begins to see the surrounding world in a distorted and fragmented manner, outside the strictures of geometric perspective.[16] Wide-angle shots of the group at play intermingle with details relating to a particular woman—a white summer hat, polka dots on light fabric, a hand holding a wild flower. She is the mother (Silvana Mangano), and the infant's keenest attention is directed toward her. Then, as the rhythm dilates, a shot of the child sucking at his mother's breast is followed by a prolonged close-up of the woman's face, and a slow, fluid take on the overhanging poplars. Both the face and the landscape, here metonymically linked through the child's look, become visible "as if for the first time." The mother's mutable expressions—serene, perturbed, reassured, amused—reappear in the light vibrating amid the foliage, the sound of rustling leaves, the density of the sky. The poplars are now almost within

our reach, the distance between them and our eyes having been reduced
through the adoption of a long lens, and we most intensely experience
the "strange possession" which Merleau-Ponty describes, that "having at
a distance" which constitutes vision.[17] No longer static, as in front of the
mother's face, the camera traces what feels like a gesture of the body—a
lingering eye movement along the highest branches—and then returns to
the ground. As in Cézanne's paintings, we are offered "the impression of
an emerging order,"[18] the spontaneous gathering together of colors and
forms, the birth of desire through the body's silent laboring.

Much later, led by a youngster with spirited eyes and black curls
(Ninetto Davoli), a blind man (Franco Citti) walks through the square
and the countryside that had marked the beginning of the film. As they
reach the meadow, the man stops and closes his eyes, as if to see the mass
of green leaves above him by receiving its rays of light and shadow, its
freshness and warmth, its diffuse smell.[19] It is here that the long take on
the poplars returns, exactly as it appeared following the close-up on the
mother's face. Once more, in the tension between proximity and distance generated through the long lens and a panning, almost handheld
camera, we partake of that vision which is "palpation with the look"—
not appropriation but interlacing of the seer and the seen.[20] The blind
man too perceives the landscape he had seen as an infant, not because he
is able to remember it by withdrawing into a secluded interior space, but
because his body becomes the site where the primordial connectedness
of the senses intermingle with the thickness of the world. No longer the
object of the subject's gaze, the landscape reciprocates this strange and
familiar look. It is the enchanted experience many painters have tried
to translate into words: "In a forest, I have felt many times over that it
was not I who looked at the forest. Some days I felt that the trees were
looking at me, were speaking to me. . . . I was there, listening."[21] As
the shot ends, there where we saw the child lying on the grass, we now
see the blind man staring ahead, his face occupying the larger portion
of the screen. He asks, "Where are we?" "We are in a place with many
trees in a row and many little streams and a green, green field," is the
young man's simple answer. As if the definitive recognition of such a
unique place could only occur through the words donated to him by his
companion—language emerging as another modality of perception, not

competing with the senses but partaking of their expressivity—the blind man speaks in turn, "Oh light that I saw no more, that formerly was mine, now you illuminate me for the last time. I have arrived. Life ends where it begins." The film ends, too, here where it had begun.

As I return to the beginning and the end of the film in cyclical fashion, each time captivated by the precise resonances and poignant divergences connecting the two parts, I recognize the traits of what Pasolini himself has named "free indirect subjectivity." In the essay "The Cinema of Poetry," written shortly before the making of *Oedipus Rex*, Pasolini defines free indirect subjectivity as the cinematic version of literature's interior monologue—a complex procedure which allows the filmmaker to speak through an intermediary and, at the same time, in the first person. Situated on the level not of language but of style, it complicates the distinction between author and character, enunciation and statement, and ultimately subject and object. If, in the cinematic realm, direct discourse primarily manifests itself through the point-of-view shot, free indirect discourse mobilizes a series of devices which, without being as differentiated as those available to verbal language, can nonetheless be satisfactorily identified. Regarding the works of directors such as Antonioni, Bertolucci, and Godard, Pasolini writes:

The camera is felt and for good reasons. The alternation of different lenses . . . on the same face, the abuse of the zoom with its long focuses which adhere to things and expand them like loaves with too much yeast, the continuous and deceptively casual shots against the light which blind the camera, the tremblings of the hand-held camera, the exasperated tracking-shots, the mistakes in the editing done for expressive reasons, the irritating opening shots, the shots held interminably on the same image, etc.[22]

It is through stylistic solutions of this kind that free indirect subjectivity has begun to disarticulate cinema's historical alliance with prose, liberating that potential for poetic expression that lies buried under well-established narrative conventions. As a result, the medium's repressed attributes—its irrational, oneiric, elemental, barbaric qualities—can become visible once again.

While discussing Antonioni's *Red Desert*, Pasolini isolates a particularly significant instantiation of free indirect subjectivity, namely, the assemblage of two shots that portray the same object from similar yet nonidentical viewpoints. He writes:

The sequential juxtaposition of two viewpoints, scarcely different from each other, directed toward the same image: that is, the succession of two shots which frame the same portion of reality—first from up close, then from *a little* farther away; or else, first frontally and then *a bit obliquely*; or else, finally, actually on the same axis but with two different lenses. This gives rise to an insistence which becomes obsessive, like the myth of the real and anguishing autonomous beauty of things.[23]

Even if Pasolini illustrates the difference between the two framings in spatial terms—the camera, he specifies, moves farther away, or to the side, or switches lens while remaining still—I believe that such difference can also be construed as temporal. In *Oedipus Rex*, Pasolini himself expands our understanding of free indirect subjectivity by presenting two shots that, though literally identical and positioned at the film's opposite ends, are distinguished and simultaneously interlocked by a circular, convoluted time. The poplars leading back to the eyes of the child as well as of the blind man are technically the same, and yet they are inhabited by a difference I will attempt to describe as one of temporal density. That they are inserted in what seemingly corresponds to an eyeline match should not mislead us: in the world of primordial perception, the very distinction between subject and object of vision is dismantled, and the lived body sees only to the extent that it is seen. Here, we will discover, free indirect subjectivity does not express the viewpoint of an autonomous subject, whether character or filmmaker, a subject present to itself and grounded in the certainty of the moment. On the contrary, it realizes both the emergence and the dissolution of the subject, exposing him as the being who is subjected to a heterogeneous time and a dispersed vision.

Beyond Oedipus

The film's structure is essential to defining the difference between the identical shots of the poplars. Through a series of brilliant narrative solutions, the events of the Oedipus myth are told in chronological order, and yet linear time is radically disrupted. A contemporary narrative encloses the mythical tale, which begins when a baby with swollen feet is rescued from death, and ends when Angelo, the messenger, guides a blind and desperate Oedipus away from Thebes. Set in the desert of Northern Africa, amid tribal costumes and details reminiscent of an imaginary Greek past, this part of the film possesses an almost hallucinatory quality, and defies any attempt to situate the events in a specific time and place. Unlike the central segment, the frame narrative unfolds in twentieth-century Italy, re-creating a historically accurate environment. The prologue shows the closeness between mother and child, most strikingly in the sequence described above, as well as the jealousy and hatred which the father, a young officer during the fascist regime, experiences toward his new-born son. The epilogue portrays a blind flute player who, after wandering the streets of Bologna and the industrial peripheries of Milan, finally returns to the countryside of his childhood. Since the epilogue directly follows the Greek episode, and the actors remain unchanged throughout the film, it seems as if Oedipus and Angelo had been walking together across the centuries, under the effect of a spell or a curse.[24] Conversely, the prologue constitutes what will have been in a distant future, and yet is presented as the origin of the past. At the end as well as at the beginning, there appears to be no other time than the time of the Oedipal transgression. If the conventional detective story begins with a death that has already occurred, Pasolini's film opens with a crime that, in the socio-symbolic order marked by the Oedipus myth, will have always already been committed.

Pasolini's own words expose the intimacy between the beginning and the end of the film. In an interview with Jean Narboni, he says: "The prologue is the childhood of a little boy who could be any one of us, and who dreams the whole myth of Oedipus as it was told by Sophocles but of course with Freudian elements. At the end, the little boy is blind and old."[25] However, the last phase of Oedipus's life is not homogeneous, but unfolds in three movements or acts: Oedipus is shown playing the flute in Bologna's main square, as middle-class customers enjoy the surrounding arcades; then on Milan's gray outskirts, as workers exit the local factory; and finally returning to the village, where the course of his existence will have come full circle. Pasolini explains: "First Oedipus is a decadent poet, then a Marxist poet, then nothing at all, someone who is going to die."[26]

It is through an admirable rewriting of the original dramaturgy that such an intricate journey is made possible. Greece, according to Pasolini, is "barbaric" because it refuses any neoclassical idealization and positions itself on the side of the peasant world, the oppressed, the mother, the body.[27] Its Oedipus is profoundly anti-intellectual. If Freud had already complicated the role played by the strategies of reason, Pasolini now questions Oedipus's very desire to know. In relation to the unconscious, Oedipus is a detective who does not want to see, repeatedly covering his eyes with his left hand to shield himself against the blinding light, desperately trying to affirm his will not to know. All the fundamental encounters in his life—with the oracle at Delphi, with Laius at the fateful crossroads, with the Sphinx on the mountain overlooking Thebes—leave him frightened and confused, ready to run away in the opposite direction. Significantly, in the theatrical piece *Affabulazione* (1977; also inspired by Sophocles' tragedy), Pasolini had drawn a distinction between enigma and mystery—the former to be solved by rational cunning, the latter to be understood through the senses. Now, amid the green poplars, Oedipus does not find the last piece of a life-long puzzle—the origin of the desire which had initiated him to his destiny—but witnesses the encounter between beginning and end, their circular succession. Pasolini's Oedipus is already "beyond Oedipus," the film ending with a figure that belongs to the tragedy of *Oedipus at Colonus*—not the self-blinding king, but the wanderer, the rag picker, the poet, and, ultimately, the one who is going to die. Oedipus seen from the viewpoint of Colonus.

Shoshana Felman's reading of the difference between Freud and Lacan is in this respect illuminating. Unlike Freud, who considered the Oedipus complex as the answer to the question of unconscious desire, Lacan interprets the myth in structural terms, as a question engendered precisely by the answer that has been found. If "Freud identifies with Oedipus the King or the conqueror, the riddle solver," she claims, "Lacan identifies with Oedipus the exile (a survivor of the Plague)."[28] Lacan leaves no doubts regarding his alignment with the outcast, the one who has been excommunicated. In his seminar on the ego in Freud's theory and in the technique of psychoanalysis, he invites his listeners to go—literally—*beyond* the tragedy of *Oedipus Rex*: "You will have to read *Oedipus at Colonus*. You will see that the last word of man's relation to this discourse which he does not know is—death."[29] The discourse is that of the unconscious, the unconscious as discourse of the Other, marked by the intimate relation between the death drive and the signifier. *Oedipus at Colonus* takes us beyond Oedipus as the death drive takes us beyond the pleasure principle—until we discover that such a beyond had always been part of what it was meant to supersede. It is at this juncture that the symbolic subject, the subject qua subject of desire, can finally emerge. Lacan quotes directly from the Greek text: "In *Oedipus at Colonus*, Oedipus says the following sentence: '*Is it now that I am nothing that I am made to be a man?*' This is the end of Oedipus's psychoanalysis—Oedipus's psychoanalysis ends only at Colonus. . . . This is the essential moment which gives its whole meaning to his history."[30] By pronouncing these words, Felman explains, Oedipus goes beyond the self-recognition and self-appropriation he had realized through the gesture of self-blinding. Because true speech possesses performative and not merely constative value, Oedipus is able to face and assume his own death as inescapable possibility, in a process of self-expropriation that retroactively confers meaning on his entire existence.[31]

It is under these circumstances, that is, under the sign of the subject's confrontation with his own mortality, that free indirect subjectivity ceases to resemble a "properly cinematographic *cogito*,"[32] affirming itself as a modality of dispossessed enunciation. However, it would be inadequate to think that such a transformation occurs solely by virtue of the linguistic utterance. Oedipus's words, "life ends where it begins," are folded upon the double shot of the poplars, interweaving with the texture of perception rather than opposing it.[33] Vision is here as decentering-decentered as language and similarly endowed with performative value. Far from being a mirror in which the Cartesian subject can find evidence of his wholeness and consistency, the film's bucolic landscape testifies to a disappearance that is a dispersion of the seer into the visible—Pasolini's Oedipus being at once before and after Lacan's symbolic subject, in a relation of intimacy with the sensible world from which he had originally emerged and yet always differing from it. But what is this fissure that prevents the seer from fully merging into the seen, and the visible from coinciding with itself? Does it solely belong to space, or does it articulate itself in that "intertwining (*entrelacs*) of space and time" that Merleau-Ponty interrogates in *The Visible and the Invisible*?[34] Can we conceive of the subject's self-expropriation in relation to such a fissure—as a dissolution into a depth that is both of time and the visible?

The Face and the Landscape

The encounter between Oedipus and the meadow he has seen as a child is a source of endless fascination. It manifests a mutual and enduring recognition, a partial divergence or imperfect coincidence that cannot but dislodge traditional distinctions between subject and object, mind and matter, activity and passivity. Together with Oedipus, we find ourselves amid the visible rather than in front of it, suddenly the receivers of silent messages as well as the senders of them. In "The Cinema of Poetry," Pasolini compares our experience as film spectators to the vicissitudes of a person going for a stroll in the streets. Even if she did not hear a sound, she would still be involved in a continuous conversation with the surrounding environment—not only people, but also creatures and things would "speak" to her through their presence, which is never simple and obtuse but already immersed in a certain web of memories and desires. There is, in Pasolini's analogy, the echo of what Béla Balázs called the "mute dialogue" of people and things, the visual exchange that takes place through the expressivity of physiognomy. I am interested in exploring the contamination or promiscuity revealed by such a dialogue—in tracing the lines of the subject's disappearance as it realizes itself *through* the world's perceptual and temporal thickness, and not regardless of it. After all, Merleau-Ponty reminds us, "it is only through the world that I can leave myself."[35]

The Poetry of Things

Béla Balázs's work anticipates important issues concerning the relation between physiognomy and spectation in the age of mechanical reproduction. In "The Visible Man," first published in 1923, Balázs welcomes silent cinema as the art that will bring about the return of man's lost visibility. Our profound connections with the world of gesture, movement, and facial expression have been forgotten in the age of the printed word. It is only recently that cinema, a new technology and a new art, has restored this power to signify through the visible surfaces of our body and the world. For the first time in the modern world, "the soul and the spirit" can be "incarnated without residue,"[36] because the body and its perceptual dimensions have been rediscovered in their capacity to express a mode of existence. In the new culture inaugurated by cinema, "man has again become visible."[37]

However, Balázs emphatically states, cinema is not merely another art in the Western figurative tradition, since it defies the principle of unbridgeable distance between spectator and spectacle on which the latter is founded. Cinema presents its viewer with the possibility of traveling along the trajectory of the look, and entering the picture. It is the unique "transport or abduction" we have discussed in the previous chapter—a process of seduction that preserves rather than assimilating the other's corporeal difference. The spectator who watches a filmed version of Shakespeare's *Romeo and Juliet* finds herself drawn into the spectacle, almost compelled to leave her own look behind and adopt the characters' viewpoint. In this case, we must notice, the journey into otherness is only temporary—the spectator eventually regains her own bodily coordinates. And it is set into motion by the human form—Romeo's and Juliet's eyes are the center around which the identificatory experience revolves. But in the old Chinese tale that Balázs summarizes shortly after this discussion, if only to highlight that other cultures have long questioned the separation between the viewer and the viewed, we find the traces of a more radical self-expropriation:

There was once a painter who one day painted a landscape. It was a beautiful valley with wonderful trees and with a winding path leading away towards the mountains. The artist was so delighted with his picture that he felt an irresistible urge to walk along that path winding away towards the distant mountains. He entered the picture and followed the path towards the mountains and was never seen again by any man.[38]

Here, not only is the spectator's disappearance into the spectacle permanent—the spectacle itself, the force that has initiated the abduction, is a landscape seemingly devoid of any human presence. What the Chinese painter undergoes could be described as a dispersion into the visible world, the other with which she heteropathically identifies being in excess of any bodily ego—corresponding indeed to the landscape itself, in its indefinite regression toward the horizon line.

"We are in the picture," Balázs writes. For the first time in the history of Western art we find ourselves amid a scene unfolding on a two-dimensional surface. But what kind of visual life have we entered, what is our position in the cinematic picture? We are in the picture with things that we do not treat from the vantage point of a privileged position. There is no special place for human beings in the texture of film, since animate and inanimate beings are made of the same material. "In the silent film both man and object were equally pictures, photographs, their homogeneous material was projected on the same screen, in the same way as in a painting, where they are equally patches of color and equally parts in the same composition. In significance, intensity and value men and things were thus brought on to the same plane."[39] The discovery of this commonality does not deprive human beings of the expressivity of their bodies. On the contrary, it allows them to establish a more profound relation with things, to cross the reductive boundaries within which their subjectivity had been confined. At the same time, things do not appear as inaccessible and inexpressive entities, but reveal a life which had until then remained hidden. Cinema, Balázs writes, finally discloses their face, allows them to show their physiognomy. The fact that "our anthropomorphous world-vision makes us see a human physiognomy in every phenomenon,"[40] however, derives less from an imposition of subjective qualities onto objects than from the recognition that human beings and things are made of the "same stuff."[41]

The camera has the capacity to reveal the "the hidden life of things" because there is a profound permeability between the body and the world. Not only is the world familiar with our corporeality, but it also bears the traces of our incarnate existence, the mark of our particular corporeal styles. What Balázs calls the "poetry of things" is the appearance of this intertwining between worldly forms and human feelings or thoughts. The camera has the power to unveil a world that speaks of our secret moods, our unconscious states of mind, thus presenting us with aspects of our own being which would otherwise go unnoticed. Above all, the close-up can "show the face of things and those expressions on them which are significant because they are reflected expressions of our own subconscious feeling."[42] Love, hate, tenderness, and anguish find their expression not only on the faces of the people experiencing them, but also in the social and natural environment in which they are immersed: "The expression of the human face radiates beyond the outline of the face and is repeated in the images of furniture, trees or clouds."[43] Through close-ups, but also through camera angles and changing setup, we are given a world of things, a landscape that speaks of our affects and unconscious ideas. It is because we relinquish our autonomy and control, and recognize the bond which links us to the world, that "we rejoice in the landscape which looks back at us with friendly and intelligent recognition, as if calling us by name."[44] We become the receivers of a look that comes from outside, from a world which is anthropomorphous only to the extent that we are of this world, and can express ourselves only in it.

The Flesh (Narcissism)

There are multiple resonances between Balázs's theory of film and Merleau-Ponty's phenomenology. In "The Film and the New Psychology," Merleau-Ponty celebrates cinema in its capacity to "make us see" what phenomenology and modern psychology painstakingly describe: our constitutive involvement with people and things. The spectacle of cinema, like the spectacle of the world, lets thoughts and feelings emerge as modes of behavior, ways of inhabiting space and performing certain movements. The essay ends with a phrase that is at once precise and enigmatic: "What is inside is also outside."[45] In the writings on painting which I have approached at the beginning of this chapter, Merleau-Ponty describes our enmeshment in the world with respect to the reflexivity of the sensible, the reversibility between the seer and the seen which transforms us into the recipients, and no longer only the bearers, of the look. Yet it is Merleau-Ponty's last, unfinished text that, further developing the questions posed in "Eye and Mind," offers us the invaluable blueprint for understanding the subject's dissemination into the visible and its mysterious depth. The cohesion between people and things of which Balázs speaks will find its most complex interpretation in Merleau-Ponty's ontological project.

In *The Visible and the Invisible*, Merleau-Ponty sets out to interrogate what traditional philosophy has not yet named—the flesh of the
world. Neither mind nor matter, the flesh is an "element," in the sense
that water, air, earth, and fire were elements for the pre-Socratic philoso-
phers: not things in themselves but "rhizomata," the roots of all things.
It is not any particular thing, then, but a "general thing"; not a thing
which can itself be present in the here and now, but that which lets all
things exist in a certain space, at a certain time. The flesh is an "'element'
of Being," the "incarnate principle" that allows all beings to be,[46] "the
formative medium of the object and the subject."[47] He writes: "When
we speak of the flesh of the visible . . . we mean that carnal being, as a
being of depths, of several leaves or several faces, a being in latency, and
a presentation of a certain absence, is a prototype of Being, of which our
body, the sensible sentient, is a very remarkable variant, but whose constitutive paradox also lies in every visible."[48] Being the "stuff" of which
all visibles are made, the flesh is endowed with a paradoxical reflexivity,
which characterizes every visible and which our body most impressively
exemplifies: the reversibility between the seer and the seen. It is easier,
Merleau-Ponty suggests, to comprehend the dynamics of this encircle-
ment if we consider touch, and the fact that it is in one and the same
movement that my right hand touches my left hand and is touched by it.
As the body can touch only because it is also tangible, the body can only
see because it is also visible—because it is caught in the general visibility
of the flesh. In itself invisible, the flesh allows the body to simultaneously
appear and see, to see itself seeing.[49]

It is in relation to the ultimate notion of flesh and its impersonal
character that Merleau-Ponty redefines the concept of narcissism. Vision
comes into being when the visible circles back upon itself, when the
body and the visible from which it emerges face each other as two mir-
rors reflecting images that could not be assigned to any single one of
them, being the product of their coupling and differentiation. Here, the
mirror is affirmed as the instrument or added organ that doubles and
displays the anonymous labor of vision. A "technique of the body," it
is at once the mark of externality and nonpossession, to the degree that
the flesh itself, Merleau-Ponty will note, can be thought of as "a mirror
phenomenon."[50] Far from distinguishing a unilateral and punctual look,

narcissism comes to coincide with the constitutive and paradoxical reflexivity of the flesh:

Thus since the seer is caught up in what he sees, it is still himself he sees:
there is a fundamental narcissism of all vision. And thus, for the same reason,
the reason he exercises, he also undergoes from the things, such that, as many
painters have said, I feel myself looked at by the things, my activity is equally
passivity—which is the second and more profound sense of the narcissism: not
to see in the outside, as the other sees it, the contour of a body one inhabits,
but especially to be seen by the outside, to exist within it, to emigrate into it,
to be seduced, captivated, alienated through the phantom, so the seer and the
visible reciprocate one another and we no longer know which sees and which
is seen.[51]

Since the seer is part of the fabric of the world—her body made of the
same stuff the world is made of—it is the reflection of herself as other
that she sees when she looks at the world. But it also happens that the
activity of her look is turned upon itself, transformed into a mystery of
passivity. Suddenly, the seer finds herself being looked at, not by her own
narrow look mirrored on a flat surface, but by the look of the things
around her.[52]

The self "by narcissism" that, in "Eye and Mind," Merleau-Ponty
opposes to the *cogito* is thus thoroughly carnal and fundamentally decentered—a self engrossed in things, but also a self of which things are
part. It is by virtue of such a confusion that Balázs's spectator can be
drawn into the picture as into a spectacle which is not extraneous to
her. Rather than representing an obstacle, the thickness of the visible
is what makes this abduction possible, what allows the self to be inherently other—alienated and absent from itself. Indeed, in the realm of
wild or brute perception, which painting as well as cinema rediscover,
"there is . . . no problem of the *alter ego* because it is not *I* who sees,
not *he* who sees, because an anonymous visibility inhabits both of us,
a vision in general."[53] Like the subject of language, spread through the
interstices of a diacritical system that precedes and exceeds her, the subject of perception emerges here as "nobody,"[54] her vision entangled in
the internally differentiated and impersonal mass which Merleau-Ponty
has called flesh. Ultimately, the face and the landscape—Oedipus's face

and the landscape of his infancy—do not compete, as if to conquer the position from which vision is mistakenly believed to originate, nor merge into a homogeneous being, but mirror each other in a play of proximity and distance. The attempt to show that such a reciprocal engagement transcends the order of space will lead me to explore the final section of Merleau-Ponty's seminal project.

The Poetry of Time

In the "Working Notes" to *The Visible and the Invisible*, Merleau-Ponty discloses an intimate connection between the reversibility of the flesh and a temporality that defies the metaphysical model of presence.[55] He writes, "past and present are . . . each enveloping-enveloped—and that itself is the flesh."[56] Like the flesh, time is a "chiasm,"[57] the intertwining of dimensions that are never autonomous. Indeed, there is no certainty of the present which can be established from beneath or outside the flow of time: "the new present is itself transcendent: one knows that it is not there, that it was just there, one never coincides with it—It is not a segment of time with defined contours that would come and set itself in place. It is a cycle defined by a central and dominant region and with indecisive contours."[58] What emerges is a time that always turns back upon itself, connecting past and future through multiple reversals and continuous infiltrations. The past was not once and for all. Instead, it cannot stop having been and returns in the future as it has been transformed by the future itself. However, there is no fusion between past and future, just as there is no coincidence between my body and the world, seer and seen. On the contrary, Merleau-Ponty reminds us, there is always a fission or *écart* between them: "it is time to emphasize that it is a reversibility always imminent and never realized in fact. My left hand is always on the verge of touching my right hand touching things, but I never reach coincidence."[59] Difference is of perception as it is of time.

Like the flesh, time is in excess of the subject. It cannot be arranged according to geometric coordinates, divided into segments and measured as if it were inert matter—it cannot be spread out before a disembodied mind. Its internal proliferation can only be made visible, always imperfectly and by degrees. Like the flesh, time is endowed with an inexhaustible depth, and characterized by several sheets. What we see, the so-called "here and now," is only the ostensible counterpart of the invisible and of other moments of time: "Like the memory screen of the psychoanalysts, the present, the visible counts so much for me and has an absolute prestige for me only by reason of this immense latent content of the past, the future, and the elsewhere, which it announces and which it conceals."[60] The landscape that is around us does not relate to other places and other times in an external and sequential manner, but holds them "inside" or "behind" itself, simultaneously—caught within the flesh of time, it is always different from itself.[61] "Even in the present," Merleau-Ponty writes, "the landscape is a configuration."[62] The present, the visible, is the reverse or doubling of the past, the future, and the invisible. The poplars and the meadow to which Pasolini returns in *Oedipus Rex* secrete—that is, at once radiate and withhold—the vicissitudes of a desire that permeates our history: "like the memory screen of the psychoanalysts," Merleau-Ponty says. And because screen memories, in Freud's words, "represent the forgotten years of childhood as adequately as the manifest content of a dream represents the dream-thoughts,"[63] we might dare consider the dream too, together with the landscape, not as a picture puzzle but as a "configuration." This is the undoing of the detective story, the unraveling of psychoanalysis as detection. Yet, how can we conceive of such a configuration, now that the boundaries of subject and object have been dismantled?

It is at this juncture that Merleau-Ponty's call for "an *ontological* psychoanalysis," for an interpretation of Freud's philosophy as a "philosophy of the flesh,"[64] becomes most fascinating. In the philosophy of the flesh, there is a profound affinity between the invisible and the unconscious. Indeed, Merleau-Ponty first identifies the unconscious with the unseen ground against which the figure (the conscious) comes into relief,[65] then with the invisible itself—not the opposite of the visible, but its "secret counterpart," its "inner framework."[66] As the invisible, the unconscious is outside, in the midst of things rather than at the center of the psyche: "This unconscious is to be sought not at the bottom of ourselves, behind the back of our 'consciousness,' but in front of us, as articulations of our field. It is 'unconscious' by the fact that it is not an *object*, but it is that through which objects are possible, it is the constellation wherein our future is read."[67] Both the invisible and the unconscious are "existentials"—neither objects nor persons, but structures that make possible the exchange between self and world, self and other. Every visible partakes of this double texture, whose reverse side is like "the finger of the glove that is turned inside out" and can thus be accessed each time one sees or touches the obverse side.[68] However, because the invisible or the unconscious are more than a background that could be converted into a figure by shifting focus, every visible is also the index of a permanent reserve of invisibility, of an unconscious that is never available to complete disclosure.

Merleau-Ponty writes that a certain visible, for instance a certain red, is not a thing I either see or do not see, but the opening, within the field of my vision, of myriad connections. This red is connected with other reds, with other colors, with the red things I have once seen or imagined; it is part of a certain "constellation" of reds. A simple red dress, for instance, is "a punctuation in the field of red things, which includes the tile of roof tops, the flags of gatekeepers and of the Revolution, certain terrains near Aix or in Madagascar, it is also a punctuation in the field of red garments," and so on, indefinitely.[69] Since, as Merleau-Ponty suggests, both language and perception are diacritical,[70] we could think these constellations as "articulations" of the flesh—as visible configurations of an impersonal visibility, of a latent or oblique vision capable of engendering a seeing that is not mine alone—a vision that holds different temporal dimensions in a relation not of succession but of simultaneity. Merleau-Ponty defines the constellations of images constituting our vision through a metaphor which invites us to rethink the relation between memory, the subject, and the world: "the 'associations' of psychoanalysis," he writes, "are in reality 'rays' of time and of the world."[71] The expression "Memory of the World," which appears in the "Working Notes" without forming a complete sentence,[72] voices this profoundly visual intertwining of past, present, and future—a depth which is at once of the visible and of time.

In Pasolini's *Oedipus Rex*, this memory permeates the surface of the screen as well as its invisible counterpart. At its highest degree of concentration in the returning shots of the poplars, it is not only in excess of Oedipus's subjectivity—it is that from which Oedipus emerges as a tentative, primordial I or point of view, into which he fades as a symbolic subject. Here, in the meadow that will see him for the last time—in the meadow that saw him for the first time—Oedipus is not yet and no longer an eye/I. He appears—the most passive of constitutions—because he is seen or touched by a time that is flesh and memory of the world, and into this time he disappears, like the painter who becomes painting. The journey to Delphi, the encounter with Laius at the crossroads, the confrontation with Tiresias—but also the crown of pink flowers he wears as a youngster, the blue cloak and the golden jewels adorning Jocasta, the white shells shaping the Sphinx's mouth—they are all here, in the vibrating green of the leaves, not as traces of the past or intimations of the future, but as the other side of the landscape we see, its secret constellation. For Oedipus and the spectator who feels caught in the same flesh of time, this is the most tender and the most terrible of sights.

4

Twilight

> In this matter of the visible, everything is a trap, and
> in a strange way—as is very well shown by Maurice
> Merleau-Ponty in the title of one of the chapters of
> *Le Visible et l'invisible—entrelacs* (interlacing, intertwining).
> There is not a single one of the divisions, a single one
> of the double sides that the function of vision presents,
> that is not manifested to us as a labyrinth.
>
> Jacques Lacan[1]

The Line and the Labyrinth

The Cretan labyrinth is a classical labyrinth—you enter through the mouth and, walking along its paths or circuits, eventually reach the center. Once you are there, you have gone half the distance; now you need to turn around and retrace your steps—in a preordained reversal, the entrance will become the exit and let you out. I have seen this pattern reproduced on Cretan coins dating back to 500 B.C., but also on the floors of Roman buildings and in numerous medieval churches. The center is at times occupied by the Minotaur, and more often by a blank or a void. John Ruskin, preeminent art critic of the Victorian age, compares the designs appearing on two Cretan coins to the labyrinth sculpted on the eastern side of the Cathedral of Saint Martin in Lucca, and notes that "a single path or track, coiled, and recoiled, on itself" characterizes all of them. As if defining the sign under analysis entails laying bare the rules for its approximate duplication, he then supplies the reader with precise directives: "take a piece of flexible chain and lay it down, considering the chain itself as the path: and, without interruption, it will trace any of the three figures."[2] Ruskin's insistence on the term *path*, in addition to his translating the word *labyrinth* as "rope-walk" or "coil-of-rope-walk," suggest that the self-encircling line I see is more than a configuration to be observed from outside. Perfectly and deceptively symmetrical, this line exercises a pull or magnetic attraction that draws my body within its loops, at once affirming vision as a way of inhabiting the visible, and the visible as a potential trap.

The simplicity of the classical labyrinth has generated disparate responses. Writing the preface to an erudite book, Umberto Eco proposes to organize the innumerable forms that have marked the history of the labyrinth according to three models.[3] The first model, epitomized by the Daedalian labyrinth, includes designs made of a single course, that is, lacking knots and even bifurcations. No matter how intricate the path appears to the eye that contemplates it from above, such a labyrinth is like a skein of wool with two ends—once untangled, it becomes a straight, uncomplicated line. The Minotaur stands in the center as the bearer of a possible alternative—after all, my destiny has come to a crossroads. Here, Eco points out, the question is not "from which side shall I exit?" but "shall I get out?"—that is, "shall I get out alive?" The symbol of a cosmos in which each encounter will likely turn into a deadly confrontation, the classical labyrinth nonetheless reveals an underlying order and, so to speak, can be brought to reason. Does not Theseus, hero of Apollonian clarity, finally conquer the labyrinth, dissipating its obscurity by means of a thread?

In Eco's account, true complexity only resides in the two latter models. The second model is that of the mannerist labyrinth, which unfolds not into a thread but into a treelike structure, an arboreal pattern offering countless ramifications and merely one viable option. While there is a risk that one might lose oneself endlessly, in principle such a labyrinth is governed by a rule that may be learned by advanced calculations. The third model, on the other hand, consists of an infinite net or rhizome—a maze without fixed partitions, open to incessant and unpredictable alterations, where even the distinction between inside and outside results nullified. Eco visualizes it through the image of a buttery mass, boundless and malleable, but also compares it to "a book in which every reading changes the order of the letters, thus producing a new text."[4] In the light of the tripartite classification just delineated, it is this last analogy that I find more provocative.

Text and interpretation, labyrinth and thread stand here in a relation that defies both chronology and causality, the text existing as that which will have been transformed by the interpretation it engenders, always in the process of becoming (other than) itself. If reading according to the rhizome is but a mode of rewriting, are we then to consider the classical labyrinth as the promise or threat of a literal course—a story line we can dutifully retrace, a text we can decipher once and for all? Or is its simplicity the mark of an irreducible and ever proliferating complexity?

At the end, as J. Hillis Miller reminds us in *Ariadne's Thread*, Theseus does not triumph over the maze. After abandoning Ariadne, he reaches the island of Delos and there pays tribute to Apollo and Aphrodite by way of a dance. Performed by the young men and women he rescued in Crete, "the dance of Theseus" comprises intricate and winding movements—the return of the Dionysian turmoil, the repetition of a pattern he could not leave behind. This strange intimacy between labyrinth and thread is reaffirmed in the legend of Daedalus and the seashell. Daedalus, the architect and inventor who provided Ariadne with the knowledge of the thread, eventually finds refuge in Sicily and there lives incognito until Minos lures him into a trap. Traveling from town to town, the king promises a reward to anyone who could confront a seemingly innocent problem—how to run a thread through all the twists and turns of a seashell. Daedalus punctures the center of the elaborate shell, ties a thread to an ant, places the ant inside, and waits. When the ant reemerges, not from the artificial perforation but from the shell's mouth, Daedalus is at once victorious and ensnared.

I look again at the illustrations depicting the Cretan coins and the slab of stone on the Lucca cathedral, waiting for my entrapment to resume its course. The line I now see on their surface—the single path which constitutes the labyrinth's secret shape and the sought-after key to its unraveling—is, to adopt Ruskin's formulation, at once "simple and complex." As Miller brilliantly argues, this line disrupts its own linearity by repeating itself, turning back on its own course and engendering figures not of mere discontinuity but of confusion: "returnings, knottings, recrossings, crinklings to and fro, suspensions, interruptions."[5] Repeatedly tangled, perversed, troubled—destined to reproduce its intricacy each time an act of disentanglement is initiated—this line resists the inquiry of the distant eye. Indeed, Ariadne's thread can function as a "clue" only after you have entered the labyrinth and started walking between its walls, toward that central chamber where the "monster in midweb" is known to hide. But, as you proceed, the thread you believe to be firmly in your hands has already begun to weave, transforming you into a spider and becoming itself another web. That is—the clue has already begun to mime the puzzle it is meant to solve, and the investigator to dangerously identify with the criminal she is pursuing (or the victim she is attempting to rescue). What is this strange metamorphosis, occurring by means of a necessary but self-effacing clue, which ultimately leads the detective not to solve the riddle but to dissolve into it?

Seldom has anyone written of the line and the labyrinth as perfectly as has Jorge Luis Borges. Short, exact, infinitely faceted—possessing what Italo Calvino has called "the rigorous geometry of the crystal"[6]— Borges's fictions often rely on the detective story to articulate vertiginous models of the universe. While foregrounding the rules of the genre, they establish a parallel between detection and textual interpretation, and invariably affirm both as the site of a multiple, decentered, austerely imaginative existence. In "Death and the Compass," a mixture of scrupulousness and audacity leads the protagonist—"a reasoning machine, an Auguste Dupin," but also a bit of a gambler—right into the labyrinth woven by his opponent. Here, the corpse which counts the most appears not at the beginning but at the end, and coincides with the corpse of the reader's most visible representative, the detective himself—always on the verge of being hit by a lethal bullet, always never quite dead.[7] In "The Garden of the Forking Paths," a tale of espionage that is also a treatise on time, the protagonist discovers that the garden, the book, and the labyrinth to which a famous ancestor had devoted his final years are indeed one and the same, namely, a labyrinth not of space but of time, "a growing, dizzying web of divergent, convergent, and parallel times."[8] Again, this knowledge comes to him as he resolutely prepares to die, the last of three stupefying hypotheses on the nature of time. "First there is an idea of precise time, almost an absolute, subjective present," Calvino writes, expanding upon few condensed lines. "Then there is a notion of time as determined by the will, in which the future appears to be as irrevocable as the past; and finally the central idea of the whole story—a manifold and ramified time in which every present forks out in two futures."[9] It is this heterogeneous time—a time that can be thought and experienced only as a labyrinth—that at once constitutes and disperses protagonist, narrator, and reader alike.

The extent to which the dissolution of uniform time poses a challenge to interpretation, inducing us to reconsider the question of truth so central to detective fiction, emerges most clearly in Borges's "The Theme of the Traitor and the Hero." A detective story, an essay on historiographical writing, and a family romance, this short text mobilizes a flawlessly orchestrated variety of metaphors. The protagonist is the reader of a hidden plot, the writer of a biography, the foreseen character in a play that has not ended, the guardian of his great-grandfather's legacy. The labyrinth is a spider's web, a crime scene, a theatrical performance, the space of a city, history itself. The line is a thread, a clue, a narrative line, a genealogical line, the line of perspective—a figure bound to turn into another labyrinth, another "pattern of repeating lines."[10] The final discovery that the protagonist's ancestor was not a hero but a traitor is as perfectly ambiguous as the story that leads to it, an incomplete story, partially unknown to the very narrator who has conceived it, a story that meticulously avoids telling the details of the investigative process that should constitute its core. How can one find the truth, and which truth is to be found, in a maze inescapably raised to the second power?

Bernardo Bertolucci's *The Spider's Stratagem*, freely adapted from "The Theme of the Traitor and the Hero," dramatizes and complicates the vicissitudes of the repeating line, transferring Borges's time labyrinth from the domain of language to that of vision. As I move toward this enigmatic film, determined to understand the truth of a crime scene that spans more than two generations—the diegetic present is 1970, but the stratagem was once woven in 1936 and is now reaching down to me—I choose to follow a thread that is already double. On the one hand, I will elaborate on Lacan's notion of full speech and the alternative to referential truth it proposes. This notion is most valuable to me because, in privileging speech over discourse, it makes it impossible to separate the truth from the time of its appearance, indeed from time itself. Not any single temporal dimension, but the future anterior as the intertwining of past and future is the time of full speech. On the other hand, I will ask, does language constitute the only domain in which full speech can be realized? Can there be perceptual full speech? How can one speak the truth in the field of vision? By focusing on those sequences that make visible the intermingling of day and night—the "twilight" for which the cinematography has been highly celebrated—I intend to show that *The Spider's Stratagem* succeeds in articulating the temporality of the future anterior as the chiasm of light and darkness.

The Spider's Stratagem: The Truth of the Crime Scene

"Tara": the fake plantation of *Gone with the Wind*, an imaginary town in northern Italy, and the ideal city built under the auspices of Vespasiano Gonzaga in the 1580s and officially known as Sabbioneta. As the film opens and a train enters a station marked by the sign "Tara," I wonder where I am being led. Not to any punctually present, self-identical location, I begin to suspect, but to a place that is already a constellation of memories and desires—a place in time rather than space. In the daylight, a young sailor and a man with a suitcase descend from the train and exit the station walking along parallel paths. Then the sailor stops and the other man continues to walk, until he reaches the old town center. While we still ignore his name and the details of his face, three consecutive images make us familiar with the name and appearance of yet another man. A street sign, a cultural center, and a bust—all bearing the same inscription, "Athos Magnani." On the bust, the name is followed by an epitaph, "hero vilely murdered by fascist bullets." Then, as the traveler stands still in front of the street sign, the back of his head turned to us, the camera swiftly reveals the words "Via Athos Magnani," from the traveler's point of view; by panning from right to left, uncovering the caption in reverse, the camera creates the effect of a movement that belongs to the order of time. When, in the next scene, we learn that the traveler is also named Athos Magnani,[11] and that he is returning to the town where his father was murdered more than thirty years earlier, the camera movement is retrospectively interpreted as a prelude to Athos's journey back in time. Like the backward disclosing of the street sign, which acquires meaning only after the camera has exposed all of its letters, Athos's journey will unveil the history secretly inscribed in his father's name through the winding of anticipation and retroaction.

The first time we are given a close-up of Athos's face (the actor is Giulio Brogi), he has already entered the splendid and decadent villa of Draifa (Alida Valli), the woman who has called him to Tara. Draifa was his father's lover, who, since the murder, has been living in the agony of suspended time. Indeed, the entire town seems to have fallen under a spell—deserted, enveloped in silence, inhabited only by old men who speak of the murder as if it had happened the previous day. For over thirty years, Tara has existed under the sign of what Lacan calls "formal stagnation," the rigidity which falls upon both the subject and the world when the ego successfully establishes its desire for unity and control. Athos Magnani is forever, in a perpetual present, the "hero vilely murdered by fascist bullets," and the memory of his death persists like those "embalmed forms in which myths are presented in our story-books."[12] Now his son has returned and Draifa wants him to determine what really happened in 1936 and find the man who murdered her lover. Is this an attempt to dissolve the spell and restore the flow of time? When Draifa leads Athos to stand beside his father's portrait to contemplate their extraordinary resemblance, I begin to doubt that, in her case at least, the spell will ever be broken. For a few seconds, Athos acquires the stillness of the portrait—seen through Draifa's eyes, he nearly turns into the perfect double of a dead man.

At the end of their first encounter in this "villa of optical illusions,"[13] where a series of trompe l'oeil landscapes and carefully aligned door frames confuses the distinction between inside and outside, Draifa faints and falls to the ground, silently and almost unseen by the camera. Athos, who has been walking ahead toward the exit, turns and steps back to help her. In a stylistic choice that recurs several times during the film, the camera tracks laterally to follow the character's movement but fails to register it in its totality, remaining instead out of sync with it, always too early or too late with respect to its unfolding. When Athos finally lays Draifa on a small sofa and speaks to her, a cut has already positioned us, not only in a room we do not recognize, but also in a time that is not continuous with that of the previous scene. While the dinner Athos and Draifa shared took place in full daylight, and the fainting incident lasted only a few minutes, their verbal exchange now occurs against the background of a dark, nocturnal courtyard. To the spatial confusion of the villa and its landscape, and the uncertainty of a space shaped by unorthodox camera movements, is added a temporal disorientation—a bewilderment that, I will claim, is simultaneously of time and light.

Though the editing around the fainting incident stands as the film's only abrupt transition from day to night, nevertheless the crossing of light and darkness, the intersecting of night and day that has temporarily found its center in Draifa's loss of consciousness, will return several times in a condensed form. Outside the hotel, before Athos is mysteriously locked inside a barn and left with just a match to illuminate his pitch-black surroundings, this chiasm of light and darkness emerges as a light that is irreducibly twilight—a light not of contrast but of intermingling, the inherently impure and yet crystalline light that pervades the atmosphere both after sunset and before sunrise. Bertolucci describes it as "a nocturnal light full of azure reflections, the light of those nights in which you can see everything,"[14] but we will soon discover that the most peculiar property of this light is to both display and conceal the figures it envelops. Over and over, as if Magritte's *The Empire of Light* had cast its enigmatic mood on the entire film, the distinction between light and darkness, night and day—and, ultimately, past and future—will be rendered ambiguous. That such ambiguity is never resolved is what prevents the encounter of light and darkness from turning into an affirmation of absolute light, a triumph of presence. It would be impossible to split the chiasm without destroying vision itself.

The morning after the episode of the barn, Athos is knocked unconscious. Like the hard-boiled detective, he experiences a loss of consciousness that crucially marks his involvement in the entire affair, leaving him incapable of withdrawing at will. Despite his declared intentions, he returns to the villa. There, at the end of a series of archways and communicating rooms, he finds Draifa waiting for him, as she arranges her beloved dahlias, a ritual as much as a domestic routine. To the question, "what was my father like?" she answers with a seemingly lighthearted description, "funny, very funny." The flashback that follows—the film's first flashback, a flashback from which Draifa is noticeably absent, almost an assertion of the film's own seeing power—shows Athos Magnani and his closest friends (Costa, Rasori, and Gaibazzi) wandering along a country road, immersed in twilight. Athos Magnani is wearing a pair of white trousers, a desert jacket, and a red scarf, and he is as young as his own son will have been when the flashback is triggered, while his friends are wearing dark clothes and are as old as they will have been when they meet Athos. Remarkably, each character, including father and son, is played by the same actor in the diegetic present and in the recollected past. "This is daytime, and I will prove it to you," is the challenge Athos Magnani presents to his incredulous companions. Then, while pacing around in a circle, he imitates the rooster's cry, causing the roosters to crow back from the sleepy countryside. Throughout the sequence, the camera follows or precedes his movements, like an imperfect double, revealing a landscape that is enfolded in twilight and punctured by distant bonfires—restless points of light returning Athos Magnani's look.

What is at stake in this apparently marginal, anecdotal flashback? That light—the unique and irreducible light of twilight—plays a pivotal role in this film of unusual perceptual intensity at the level of both diegesis and enunciation. On the one hand, the joke represents an occasion to expose Athos Magnani as a maker of artifices, a creator of fictions, and thus works as an anticipation of his political scheming. Not the truth, but its consequences do count, Athos Magnani will be recalled to say—here, the performative value of his assertion is doubled by a gesture of mimicry, the imitation of the rooster's cry, that produces a response, exercises an effect on the surrounding world, awakening it from its placid sleep. On the other hand, the flashback irrevocably connects truth and light—not the clear light of the sun or of the mind, but the "diminished," dim light of the crepuscular and auroral world.[15] This coincidence exceeds the domain of diegesis, affirming itself as an instance of cinematic enunciation. Twilight is the light and time of ambiguity, of internal difference, of perceptual play. Inexorably, it will return to mark the sequences that most effectively ask the question of truth. In these sequences, the film's twilight will appear not as background or diegetic device but, I will claim, as an act of perceptual full speech—the light or time in which the truth will have at once revealed and concealed itself. "Where are we and what time is it?" is the question protagonist and spectator alike cannot help formulating as they are asked to approach the truth and discover "la vera trama," the true woof or plot woven by the murdered hero. That such truth can no longer be conceived independently of artifice, that it lies neither behind nor ahead but in the temporality of the future anterior, that after all it corresponds to a question of creativity—the creativity of language and vision—is what Lacan's notion of full speech will allow us to determine. Yet, as I double the film's labyrinth with the convoluted thread of Lacan's theory, I will find that more threads are required. Not to exit the labyrinth, but to become one.

Speaking (in) the Future Anterior

In "The Function and Field of Speech and Language in Psychoanalysis," Lacan addresses full speech as it emerges in the domain of language. Drawing on and at the same time distancing himself from Saussurean linguistics, Lacan conceives the linguistic system or *langue* as a network of signifiers whose meaning is never simply present and fully available to its speakers. In an unfolding chain of signifiers, signification is never realized at any given moment but always anticipated in relation to the signifiers yet to be uttered. Only with the completion of a given segment of discourse, a (temporarily) fixed signification is retroactively conferred upon the various elements of the chain. Similarly, every *parole* acquires its meaning from previously spoken acts of *parole* which, at this moment—that is, retroactively—can be seen as having produced, in an anticipatory way, the final signification. Thus the word, already conceived as "a presence made of absence,"[16] can never be entirely present in itself, available for a speaker who will use it and then return it to the linguistic system as it was before, without consequences for the significations yet to come. Full speech originates from the assumption of this language that refers back to itself not as it was but as it will have been in the process of producing new significations—a language inhabiting the temporality of the future anterior. The subject who comes to full speech is called, not once and for all but over and over again, to speak a language that is other than himself, a language that preexists him and yet is always ahead of him. The opposition between full and empty speech is articulated in relation not to different languages but to different ways of speaking the same language. Empty speech is constituted by utterances that transmit a certain amount of information, without posing a question to the other nor caring for his response. Empty speech confirms the subject in his illusion of possessing a stable and coherent identity. The subject who utters it is "spoken rather than speaking,"[17] entrapped in a "frustration at a second remove,"[18] since he is not only alienated from the object of his desire but also alienated within that very object under disguise that his own ego is. Full speech, on the other hand, is posed like a question and realized through the other's response: "What I seek in speech is the response of the other. What constitutes me as subject is my question. In order to be recognized by the other, I utter what was only in view of what will be."[19] Full speech coincides with the subject's assumption of his own history, the history of his desire as subject, in the field of the other. The subject who comes to full speech abandons the frozen present of the mirror image, the temporality of an impossible wholeness, to in-habit the temporality of becoming, the intertwining of past and future which the future anterior manifests: "What is realized in my history is not the past definite of what was, since it is no more, or even the present perfect of what has been in what I am, but the future anterior of what I shall have been for what I am in the process of becoming."[20]

The future anterior that returns the subject to the temporality of becoming emerges only in relation to the limit posed to becoming itself. By speaking full speech, the subject acknowledges the lack that perpetu-ally ungrounds and, at the same time, creates his desire, the lost origin of his particular life journey toward death. The emergence of full speech coincides with the assumption of lack as finitude, of death as the authen-tic possibility of existence. Lacan writes:

The death instinct essentially express[es] the limit of the historical function of the subject. This limit is death—not as an eventual coming-to-term of the life of the individual, nor as the empirical certainty of the subject, but, as Heidegger's formula puts it, as that "possibility which is one's ownmost, unconditional, unsupersedable, certain and as such indeterminable" . . . for the subject—"subject" understood as meaning the subject defined by his historicity.[21]

Death is not a fact that has happened to others and not yet to me, but a possibility that, unlike other possibilities, I cannot avoid, beyond which nothing is possible any longer. For Lacan, profoundly inspired by Heidegger, not only is existence radically constituted by temporality, the temporality of existence cannot be thought according to the metaphysical model of simple presence. It is in the temporality of what Lacan calls "being-for-death" that the subject comes to assume the history of his desire as subject. Full speech is the manifestation of desire in a subject who lives in the anticipation of death, the revelation of a desire which is being or nothingness.[22]

What appears, with the revelation of desire in the future anterior, is truth itself. Not the truth of discourse, Lacan reminds us, but the truth of speech:

Speech appears all the more truly to be speech in that its truth is founded less on what is called "adequacy to the thing": thus, paradoxically, true speech is opposed to true discourse; their truths are distinguished by the fact that true speech constitutes the recognition by their subjects of their beings, in which they are inter-ested, whereas true discourse is constituted by knowledge of the real, in so far as the subject aims for it in objects.[23]

Whereas the truth of discourse depends on referential accuracy and revolves around the relation between subject and object, the truth of speech is *aletheia*—revelation, disclosure, unveiling—the unveiling of the subject's desire in the encounter with the other. However, since *a-letheia* is simultaneously *lethe*—occultation, concealment, veiling—true speech can also take the form of "lies, mistakes, deception, and fiction."[24] Artifice is no longer the opposite of truth, but its secret and yet most visible foil. Is the analytic setting the only domain in which such a radically transformative relationship to language can emerge? Can there be full speech outside the private sphere of psychoanalysis?

In *Seminar I*, Lacan himself suggests that transference, the intersubjective relation essential to full speech, should not be confined to the analytic domain, that "each time a man speaks to another in an authentic and full manner, there is, in the true sense, transference, symbolic transference—something takes place which changes the nature of the two beings present."[25] As a speech act, transference has an effect on both participants, whether or not they play the official roles of analyst and analysand. However, as Kaja Silverman demonstrates, it is in "The Function and Field of Speech and Language in Psychoanalysis" that Lacan conceptualizes full speech as a social, and indeed aesthetic, event. Full speech is here compared to a theatrical performance, a mise-en-scène in which the actor who speaks the lines of his own history addresses not the other but a plurality of others, namely, the chorus and the spectators. If the chorus, in its function of punctuation, can be said to occupy the structural position of the analyst, "the spectators," Silverman claims, "have no literal equivalent" in the analytic exchange.[26] They constitute an "excessive" term, a term that exceeds not only the rigorously private boundaries of analysis, but also the purely verbal nature of its dynamics. Now that a more expansive interpretation of full speech has come to the fore, can we go even further and understand full speech also as a capacity of perception? How can we say, in the domain of vision, that something "will have been"? How can we conceive of the future anterior as the time of perceptual full speech?

Perceptual Full Speech

In *The Four Fundamental Concepts of Psychoanalysis*, Lacan presents us with three diagrams—the triangle of the eye, the triangle of the gaze, and a third, more complex figure, obtained by inverting and superimposing the two triangles. As these diagrams position the subject within a field that is at once of vision and of desire, it is worth returning to them at this very juncture.[27] If the first diagram assigns the subject the geometral point or point of perspective, thus installing him as eye/I at the apex of the triangle, and the second diagram confines the subject to the side of the picture, exposing him to a gaze that is "point of light" and radical alterity, the third diagram accounts for his being simultaneously caught in both sets of relations—he looks at the object as eye/I and is looked at, photographed as picture by the gaze that is outside. I want to call attention to the fact that, despite the seeming reversibility, the point of the eye and that of the gaze are never able to coincide or exchange positions. In the third diagram, the gaze is located on the side of the object, the eye on the side of the picture. Lacan calls this composite schema an example of "interlacing, intersection, chiasma."[28] Yet, the chiasm of the eye and the gaze is a false chiasm—a figure that, while limiting the powers of the subject, imposes too strong a constraint on the articulation of the visible. Of course, the subject might want to be or believe to be the gaze. In this respect, the diagrams identify modalities of vision differently related to the subject's assumption of lack, in such a way that the distinction between full and empty speech is indirectly recalled. As a desiring subject, the seer is always already within lack. By investing his situated look with the attributes of the all-seeing gaze, the eye / I denies the nothingness of desire and grounds himself in a state of imaginary certainty. The counterpart of the Cartesian *cogito*, he apprehends perceptions in the form of representations and, like the ego vis-à-vis the mirror image, entertains with them a proprietary relationship. Geometral vision could thus be said to constitute the empty speech of the ego, the "statue" or "automaton" that, in a quest for permanence and identity, dispossesses the subject of his being and petrifies the world.[29] Then, with the appearance of the anamorphic skull, the eye / I is severed from his illusory identification with the gaze. No longer under the illusion of standing at the origin of perception, the subject discovers that the gaze is outside, on the side of things, and that he himself is first and foremost a being who is looked at, from the viewpoint of irreducible alterity. A marker or placeholder for the gaze, the skull offers us a shattering glimpse of mortality, releasing us from the suffocating immediacy of the present only to plunge us into a time in which we will have been dead. A disruption of visual Cartesianism, anamorphic vision emerges as the promise of perceptual full speech.

I say "promise" because, within the articulation of the visual field that Lacan proposes, perceptual full speech might be eluded. In Chapter 1, I questioned Lacan's ostensible stance on the geometral and claimed that perspective already contains the principle of its own implosion—that, stretched to its extreme limits, it is an apparatus capable of entrapping the subject within the reversal of viewpoint and vanishing point, thus exposing him to a temporality in excess of the present. As a result, we could argue that perspectival vision does not inevitably constitute a form of Cartesianism and empty speech, that indeed, in its impact, it approximates anamorphic vision. Yet, at this juncture, the issue I would like to pursue has a different focus: does anamorphic vision, as theorized by Lacan, constitute a form of full speech, or does it represent only its promise, its initial but restricted embodiment?

I ask such a question in the effort to venture further, beyond a subject that, while ungrounded by the emergence of the gaze, is still conceptualized in relation to the point, and discover whether a "fuller," that is, more dispersed speech is possible within the domain of perception.

Early in the seminar on the gaze, Lacan engages Merleau-Ponty's *The Visible and the Invisible* and there identifies the attempt to discover something which traditional philosophy has not yet defined: "the search for an unnamed substance from which I, the seer, extract myself. From the toils (*rets*), or rays (*rais*), if you prefer, of an iridescence of which I am at first a part, I emerge as eye, assuming, in a way, emergence from what I would like to call the function of *seeingness* (*voyure*)."[30] For Lacan, what emerges from the flesh, the luminous stuff of which both body and world are made, is the seer as eye / I or original point of vision, and what allows for such an emergence is the gaze, whose diffuse, impersonal quality sharply opposes the punctual character of the eye / I. "I see only from one point," Lacan writes, "but in my existence I am looked at from all sides." Against the grain of this idiosyncratic reading of the flesh, I will ask: is the subject's decentering-through-vision bound to be more limited than the one he attains through language? Can we think the seer as a being in radical excess of the point, indeed of any self-contained body, of any body that has ultimately been isolated from the flesh of the world? Is it possible for the seer to be not only visible from all sides but also spread out, disseminated through a multiplicity of dimensions, as he sees?

If we return to Merleau-Ponty's late work and consider again the chiasm of the seer and the seen, we will find that the seer is before and after the eye / I, in the realm of brute perception and in the world that painting or cinema can help us rediscover. Inextricably woven in the fabric of the flesh, intermingled with it, the seer is an expansive subject—a subject absorbed in things, but also a subject that things are part of. As the speaker is dispersed through language, a network of signifiers in excess of the present, so the seer is dispersed through light—the light of the flesh, the light as flesh, which for Merleau-Ponty shares language's diacritical structure. And because the flesh is also the intertwining of temporal dimensions that are neither autonomous nor coincident, the seer always sees from more than one point—in space as well as in time. From the flesh of time, he emerges as "'nobody,' in the sense of Ulysses, as the anonymous one buried in the world."[31] By rediscovering, in the impersonal visibility which inhabits him, the lack of his being and the openness of his destiny, he can speak perceptual full speech, and full speech can speak him, in the sense that "the things have us, and it is not we who have the things. . . . That language has us and that it is not who have language."[32] It is this affirmation of passivity, which is not the opposite of activity but its constitutive reversal, that will orient our interpretation of *The Spider's Stratagem* as an act of full speech performed through the texture of light and time.

Twilight Time

While Draifa, in her desire to recover the past as it was, will remain imprisoned in a petrified world, Athos will repeatedly position himself on the side of lack and eventually emerge as a figure of perceptual full speech, a seer of the past as it will have been in the interlacing of light and darkness. He has been called to the scene of a crime which he does not want to investigate—he is there to look; yet he has been constantly looked at and scrutinized since his arrival. Draifa, his father's old friends, his enemies—the entire town seems to watch over his moves. The fact of being seen by all sides profoundly disorients him, yet he does not attempt to invert the relationship and install himself in the position of the gaze. He follows, responding to the sometimes menacing, sometimes enchanting call which people and things exercise on him. And if Tara recalls a dream city, it is because the camera mimics Athos's manner of being in the visible—it also follows. The film, like Athos within its diegetic world, sees in the way we see in our dreams. "Our position in the dream," writes Lacan, "is profoundly that of someone who does not see. The subject does not see where it is leading, he follows." What does he follow? That which is being displayed by the gaze, the gaze here being not only all-seeing, but also all-showing. Even when he recognizes that it is only a dream, the subject will not be able to affirm himself as consciousness, that is, "to apprehend himself in the dream in the way in which, in the Cartesian *cogito*, he apprehends himself as thought."[33] Contrary to what Freud seems to maintain in *Interpretation of Dreams*—that the dreamer occupies central stage, asserting his egotistic desire to see—Lacan recognizes the dream as a site of decentering, of exhibitionistic rather than scopophilic tendencies.[34] Like Lacan's dreamer, Bertolucci's spectator is incessantly woven into the fabric of the visible and led to rediscover the captivating power of vision.

Toward the end of the film, Athos goes back to the railway station, determined to leave Tara and its past behind. He has been threatened not only by his father's mortal enemy but also by his father's old friends, and lured by Draifa among the vestiges of a dead world. Now, he says, this story no longer interests him. At the station, where the camera remains on the front side, we see him through the open windows and the yellow light of the waiting room, pacing along the platform in a twilight-enfolded landscape. Suddenly, the overture from Giuseppe Verdi's *Rigoletto* fills the air, diffuse and pervasive and in excess of any single source, to the point that we wonder whether it belongs to the film or to its diegetic world.[35] For Athos, this music is like a call to which he replies by walking a backward path, retracing the course that had initially led him from the station to the town center. He is arriving for the second time, doubling his own discovery of Tara in a light that is no longer daylight—he is now the Theseus of the dance, the one who explores the labyrinth by surrendering to it and taking its shape. In the twilight, Athos's purposeful movement stands out against the surreal immobility of the other listeners, elderly men and women for whom the opera is broadcasted by means of loudspeakers. Steadily, Athos follows this acoustic thread, almost a correlative of the twilight in its power to interweave different temporal dimensions, back to the alleged center of the labyrinth—the theater where his father was killed during a performance of *Rigoletto* and where Mussolini was meant to have died instead, before someone denounced Magnani and his three friends, who were planning Il Duce's assassination, to the police. An impossible center, a labyrinth in its own right.

In the theater, Athos will face Costa, Rasori, and Gaibazzi one last time and recognize that, although the story of his father's murder "looks like a fake," all the theatrics involved in the plotting (an anony-mous letter, a motorcyclist dressed in black delivering it, a gypsy read-ing the future) did not raise Athos Magnani's suspicion because he was in agreement with the three of them, his companions and assassins. As if thinking out loud, Athos draws this conclusion against the acoustic background of *Rigoletto*'s most famous aria, "Ah, La Maledizione" (Ah, the Curse) the same aria that should have covered the explosion meant to kill Mussolini and that instead ended up disguising the gunshot fired at his father. But why did the antifascist leader die in place of Il Duce, and almost in the same manner?

His father, Athos will learn, was not murdered by a fascist or a friend who betrayed him. Athos Magnani, the hero whose death is still a symbol of struggle, betrayed his friends and co-conspirators, and, when unmasked, asked to be killed in a way that would not weaken the anti-fascist cause. His death, he decided, should not be the death of a traitor, since a traitor causes damage even when he is dead—Athos Magnani should die as a "hero vilely murdered by fascist bullets," so that the peo-ple would continue to fight fascism. Accordingly, the spectacle Athos Magnani and his friends set out to perform for the citizens of Tara was that of a tragic death, a death anticipated by mysterious and yet familiar signs, which would persist in the collective imagination—the anony-mous letter, found still sealed in his pocket, warning that if he were to enter the theater that night, he would die (like Julius Caesar, before entering the senate), and the gypsy foreseeing death on the palm of his hand (*Macbeth*, the witches of prophecy).

We learn about the treachery and the extravagant murder scheme through a flashback that shows Athos Magnani first allowing himself to be questioned and beaten by his (erstwhile) friends without opposing any resistance, and then designing his own legendary death. The flash-back is positioned between the theater sequence and a sequence shot in a deserted courtyard, against the background of illuminated archways. In the courtyard, the three friends recount "what really happened" back in 1936.[36] Speaking almost directly to the camera, they remember the de-tails—the lack of time for rehearsal, the necessity to improvise, the many acts of plagiarism distinguishing the production of a theatrical event that was meant to be a perfect act of deception. However, they concur, the mechanism was faulty, because in the end someone, his son, discovered the truth. "Unless . . . ," Athos says, as the camera follows him pacing around in the twilight, tracing a circle that resembles the one drawn in the first flashback, " . . . all this had been foreseen"—unless, in an anticipatory manner, Athos Magnani himself had inscribed the forthcoming detective into his own scheme, entangled him into a web that will have remained as it was decades earlier. Now the detective is compelled to keep silent, despite his desire to shout the truth to the world.

At this crucial juncture, what binds together father and son seems to be the force of repetition as repetition of the same—a doubling that is double entrapment, persistence of the stratagem as that which is identical to itself, that which anticipates the future not to change the past. The future anterior is here the time of predetermination and closure, rather than transformation and openness to the new—everything will have already happened as such. Is this the only kind of repetition available to character and spectator alike?[37] Or does the film also confront us with the repetition of that which has never been the same, of "a past which has never been a present"[38]—a doubling that is double differentiation, turning upon the self as that which will have been other? It is through the final montage sequence, I will claim, that the film goes beyond blind repetition, offering us an exemplary act of perceptual full speech, the affirmation of truth in the future anterior. Carefully foreshadowed by the preceding shots, the sequence builds on the ambiguity of twilight and the intertwining of past and future that had pervaded the entire film, until perception and time become one single and self-differing chiasm. The impossible center of the labyrinth.

As Athos is addressing his father's three companions, a long shot of Tara in the twilight, distant amid the cornfields, punctures the scene's apparent cohesion of words and images. This shot, taken from what seems to be the viewpoint of no one, of Merleau-Ponty's "anonymous one," brings into being the montage sequence proper—an intricate arrangement of forms through which the film retraces its own steps while engendering a new course. Repetition has now become the principle of both diegesis and enunciation. At the visual level, daylight shots of the square where Athos inaugurates a memorial plaque honoring his father are edited together with fragments of previously shown flashbacks. At the acoustic level, Athos's voice as he speculates on the events continues as voice-over, intercut with the embodied voices of the characters in the flashbacks and bits of his own speech in the diegetic present. After learning what happened, Athos wonders if it is the truth—not the correct account of the events but the disclosure of their significance. As the sequence unfolds, past and future reveal their irreducible tension, allowing the truth to be unveiled in its disguise. What was—what will have been—Athos Magnani's true scheme ("la vera trama"), his hidden stratagem? Why did he encourage a conspiracy that he knew was doomed to fail? Why did he betray his companions, and then confess, only to ask that he be killed? Athos Magnani, we are led to suspect by the son's interpretive gesture, orchestrated the mise-en-scène of a mise-en-scène, so that his death would persist in the popular imagination as a call for resistance and struggle. However, since this is the truth of full speech and not of discourse, it will neither be confirmed nor supported by evidence. The sequence will not develop into the solution of the puzzle, "the end of the story [as] the retrospective revelation of the law of the whole,"[39] but will preserve the most disturbing ambiguity.

Let us consider the interaction between language and vision or, more specifically, voice and light. In the scene that immediately precedes the final montage sequence, we see Athos crossing the twilight-enfolded courtyard and hear him evaluating the information he has just received. Despite the ambiguity of the light, a certain sense of presence still saturates the scene, and the agreement of words and images only works to reinforce it. In the montage sequence, on the other hand, Athos's speech continues uninterrupted, now disembodied as voice-over rather than voice, while images of the elderly citizens gathered in celebration are intercut with glimpses of the flashbacks—Athos Magnani and Draifa on the day of their last encounter, Athos Magnani and his companions in an abandoned track, plotting the assassination of Il Duce, and later on a rooftop with a view of the entire city, plotting the death of a hero. Far from being a guarantee of objectivity and narrative authority, such a voice interrupts the coherent reasoning of the courtyard scene, while carefully avoiding the explicit formulation of an alternative hypothesis. The only complete sentences we hear are questions ("What was Athos Magnani's scheme? Who is Athos Magnani? What reason does he have to betray?"), while every potential statement remains unfinished, at times composed of mere single words ("an assassination . . . the assassins . . . an assassination doomed to fail from the beginning . . ."). By virtue of this voice, the twilight of the courtyard, which we do not see in the montage sequence, remains active as the reverse side of the light that is shown, the daylight of the flashbacks and of the diegetic present. The effect is bewildering. The past of the flashbacks and the diegetic present—what we call "now" and "then"—transform each other into the time that will have been.[40]

To make our entrapment in the labyrinth all the more compelling, the voice-over that we hear is not one. During a lull, as Athos looks over his shoulder, the film cuts to Athos Magnani on the rooftop overlooking Tara, performing the same gesture—in the foldings of time and vision, the father will have continued his son's movement, a movement that was already an imperfect repetition of his own. For a few moments, we witness Athos Magnani, almost a silhouette against the sunlight, deciding about his own death. Then, as he speaks, the film interpolates previously shown shots of the bust erected to his memory after the war and of the crowd in the diegetic present.[41] The voice-over we hear is now Athos Magnani's voice, yet the shift from the son to the father is perceived as seamless, and not simply because the same actor plays both roles—the voice-over here is not a disembodied voice but a voice that exists between bodies, between figures of different and yet interwoven times. This voice calls for the spectacle of a dramatic death, "so that people will continue to hate, and hate more and more . . . fascism." As the words are pronounced, a boy in red and then a group of boys wearing red scarves enter the square where Draifa, wearing white, and the other citizens, all dressed in black, are gathered in celebration. In this last reversal, Athos Magnani, who died in 1936, is no longer a petrified myth but the living symbol of a humanity that continues to choose its destiny.

It is Athos's daring interpretation, which coincides with the film's most convoluted operation of montage, that allows the leap from formal stagnation to perceptual full speech to realize itself. If ultimately we are led to believe that the father had indeed contrived an extraordinary scheme, it is by virtue of the performative value marking the son's perceptual utterances. In this sense, the father "will have decided" to become a traitor who poses as a hero. Through a decision that constitutes the extreme assumption of his own mortality, the ultimate affirmation of his existence, he will have been like Empedocles, who, "by throwing himself into Mount Etna, leaves forever present in the memory of men this symbolic act of his being-for-death."[42] This decision, however, is not his alone, nor does it occur in an independent temporal dimension. Father and son come to assume their own finitude in the labyrinthine time of *The Spider's Stratagem*, through an act of reciprocal limitation, an intertwining that transforms sheer rivalry into a struggle enabling both participants not to survive but to live in the anticipation of their death.

A film written in the future anterior, *The Spider's Stratagem* has already foreshadowed this transformation by doubling the encounter between Athos and his father's bust, which lies in a small square near the theater and, while in stone, displays painted features. The first encounter, immediately following Athos's arrival, takes place under the sign of direct confrontation, the two figures being positioned on a trajectory that forces them to compete for visibility. When Athos stands at the edge of the square, his back turned to the camera, what will soon be revealed as his father's bust results completely hidden, eliminated from the perceptual field. Conversely, the bust is given center stage only when Athos, who is now crossing the square, disappears behind it. To the either/or logic of this specular relation, the second encounter substitutes the irreducible tension of the chiasmatic structure. The camera shows Athos's upper body as he circles his father's bust, while in a technically surprising reverse shot the bust also appears in the act of circling, of turning upon itself as if to track Athos's movement. As a result, father and son face each other, not in a moment of stasis, in an endless and yet instantaneous duel, but in a process of sustained reciprocal motion. Instead of walking past the effigy, Athos engages it in a prolonged stare, while the bust returns his stare as it continues to gyrate, preventing Athos (and the spectator) from seeing its reverse side and experiencing a sense of mastery over the visual field. Because Athos and the statue circle together, the entrapment of father and son is reinforced but also endowed with a dynamism that offers the potential of mutual influence. Remarkably, the bust's eyes, which were originally covered with red paint and resembled the eyes of the self-blinding King Oedipus, are now white, like the eyes of the blind wanderer, Oedipus at Colonus, the one who is going to die. The scarf carved in stone, which was previously unpainted, is now red, like the one Athos Magnani always wore in life as a sign of defiance and a call for political change.

By the end of the final montage sequence, however, Athos as speaker of perceptual full speech has exceeded even the reciprocity of these two interlocked but ultimately separate bodies. He has become a figure in radical excess of any bodily ego, a figure diffused in space and time, capable of seeing and being seen from multiple viewpoints—by becoming labyrinth, he has acquired a force that is self-scattering. That we find him again at the railway station in the very last scene, next to seemingly abandoned tracks, waiting for a train whose arrival has been indefinitely postponed, is a warning against the always incumbent dangers of formal stagnation—of being rather than becoming, asserting rather than questioning. The celebration in the square has turned from an instance of entombment into an event of rejuvenation, yet such an event can only be temporary and precarious. Set outside the flow of time, separated from the creative responsibility of those who have woven it, the new stratagem runs the risk of being already old. The stratagem as a ploy existing in the present, the completed scheme, is merely that of empty speech. Because there is no original, single, and first stratagem, the spider's stratagem will have always already existed between past and future, the imperfect copy of itself as another.

In *The Visible and the Invisible*, Merleau-Ponty writes that "the flesh is not contingency, chaos, but a texture that returns to itself and conforms to itself,"[43] obliquely inviting us to interrogate the terms of this looping back. If time is the flesh or memory of the world from which I emerge and into which I disappear, the condition of a seeing that is not mine alone, then the question of return also concerns the very possibility of change. We have learned that the flesh is defined by internal scission, that it always comes back to itself as that which is different from itself—that it is more accurately described through the figure of a coiling over or folding than through the figure of a circle. And yet Pasolini's *Oedipus Rex* has shown us a flesh of time in which, despite the noncoincidence between seeing and being seeing, past and future, the weight of the past still exercises too strong a conservative influence, defining a circle that threatens to close upon itself. There, the future anterior enabled prede-termination and closure, rather than openness and transformation, to the extent that we could speak of a temporality of the curse. But in *The Spider's Stratagem*, before the spell of suspended time falls again on Tara and its inhabitants, the circle of time is endowed with the force of a vor-tex (a spiral, an incessant coiling) and the irreducible chiasms of percep-tion and time assume the shape of a labyrinth: a labyrinth in depth and of depth, a labyrinth from which the new can emerge.

Reference Matter

Notes

Introduction

1. See Pascal Bonitzer, "Il concetto di scomparsa" (The Concept of Disappearance), in *Michelangelo Antonioni: Identificazione di un autore* (Michelangelo Antonioni: Recognition of an Author), ed. Pascal Bonitzer (Parma: Pratiche, 1985), 2: 148–49. All translations are mine unless otherwise stated.

2. Ernst Bloch, "A Philosophical View of the Detective Novel," in *The Utopian Function of Art and Literature*, trans. Jack Zipes (Cambridge, Mass.: MIT Press, 1988), 245.

3. Ibid., 264.

4. Carlo Ginzburg, "Clues: Morelli, Freud, and Sherlock Holmes," in *The Sign of the Three: Dupin, Holmes, Peirce*, ed. Umberto Eco and Thomas A. Sebeok (Bloomington: Indiana University Press, 1983), 109.

5. Tom Gunning, "Tracing the Individual Body: Photography, Detectives, and Early Cinema," in *Cinema and the Invention of Modern Life*, ed. Leo Charney and Vanessa R. Schwartz (Berkeley and Los Angeles: University of California Press, 1995), 35.

6. Tom Gunning, "Lynx-Eyed Detectives and Shadows Bandits: Visuality and Eclipse in French Detective Stories and Films Before WWI," *Yale French Studies*, no. 108 (2005): 74.

7. Dennis Porter, *The Pursuit of Crime: Art and Ideology in Detective Fiction* (New Haven, Conn.: Yale University Press, 1981), 29.

8. Joan Copjec, "The Phenomenal Nonphenomenal: Private Space in *Film Noir*," in *Shades of Noir*, ed. Joan Copjec (London: Verso, 1993), 171; italics in original.

9. Roland Barthes, *Camera Lucida*, trans. Richard Howard (New York: Hill and Wang, 1981), 96.

10. Ibid., 96; italics in original.

11. Raymond Bellour, "The Film Stilled," *Camera Obscura*, no. 24 (September 1990): 109.

12. Barthes, *Camera Lucida*, 117.

13. Vivian Sobchack, *The Address of the Eye: A Phenomenology of Film Experience* (Princeton, N.J.: Princeton University Press, 1992), 23.

14. Maurice Merleau-Ponty, *The Visible and the Invisible*, ed. Claude Lefort, trans. Alphonso Lingis (Evanston, Ill.: Northwestern University Press, 1993), 128.

15. Maurice Merleau-Ponty, *Phenomenology of Perception*, trans. Colin Smith (London: Routledge and Kegan Paul, 1962), 422.

16. Merleau-Ponty, *The Visible and the Invisible*, 149.

17. P. Adams Sitney, *Vital Crises in Italian Cinema: Iconography, Stylistics, Politics* (Austin: University of Texas Press, 1995). In his book *The Cinema of Economic Miracles: Visuality and Modernization in the Italian Art Film* (Durham, N.C.: Duke University Press, 2002), Angelo Restivo reminds us that the phrase "vital crisis" is first adopted by Pier Paolo Pasolini in a discussion of the contradictions of neorealism.

18. Gilles Deleuze, *Cinema 2: The Time-Image*, trans. Hugh Tomlinson and Robert Galeta (Minneapolis: University of Minnesota Press, 1989), 2.

19. In Visconti's adaptation of Cain, the murderous lovers will find their end in a car crash that doubles the one in which Clara Calamai's husband had died. In *Story of a Love Affair*, the lovers plan the husband's murder only to become, once again, the guilty witnesses of a death they had both desired and yet (by accident) not directly caused.

Chapter 1: The Scene of the Crime

1. Stephen Heath, "Film Performance," in *Questions of Cinema* (Bloomington: Indiana University Press, 1981), 114.

2. *X Marks the Spot: Chicago Gang Wars in Pictures* (Chicago: Spot Publishing, 1930); Georges Bataille, book review in *Documents* 2, no. 7 (1930): 437.

3. See *Scene of the Crime*, ed. Ralph Rugoff (Cambridge, Mass.: MIT Press, 1995); and George Didi-Huberman, *La Ressemblance informe; ou, Le Gai Savoir visuel selon Georges Bataille* (The Likeness Without Form; or, Joyful Visual Knowing According to Georges Bataille) (Paris: Macula, 1995).

4. Stephen Heath, "Narrative Space," in *Questions of Cinema*, 36–37.

5. Rosalind Krauss, "A View of Modernism," *Artforum* (September 1972): 50.

6. The former being an example of classical cinema, the latter the extraordinary example of another organization of space-time, of other lines of subject formation.

7. Translated as "Blow-up," it was published in Julio Cortázar, *Blow-up, and Other Stories*, trans. Paul Blackburn (New York: Pantheon, 1963).

8. La Rochefoucauld, quoted in Louis Marin, "The Tomb of the Subject in Painting," in *On Representation* (Stanford, Calif.: Stanford University Press, 2001), 270.

9. See Marin, "The Ends of Interpretation; or, The Itineraries of the Gaze in the Sublimity of a Storm," in *On Representation*.

10. On the shot–reverse shot formation and an expanded notion of suture, see

Heath, *Questions of Cinema*; and Kaja Silverman, *The Subject of Semiotics* (New York: Oxford University Press, 1983).

11. This immobilization—it will become clear later in the chapter—needs to be understood in terms of desire. See Heath, *Questions of Cinema*, 53: "What moves in film, finally, is the spectator, immobile in front of the screen. Film is the regulation of that movement, the individual as subject held in a shifting and placing of desire, energy, contradiction, in a perpetual retotalization of the imaginary (the set scene of image and subject)."

12. It is well known that Renaissance perspective, invented by Filippo Brunelleschi and first theorized by Leon Battista Alberti, instituted a precise coincidence between the position taken up by the viewer and the position previously occupied by the painter—both partaking of the same point of view, both looking, as if through the same peephole, at a three-dimensional, rationalized, and abstract world. This world was uniformly organized around the "centric ray" extending from the "viewpoint" to the "vanishing point," that is, around the line or axis connecting the point, in space, where both painter and viewer were situated to the point, on the plane, where the painting's lines of flight converged. However, "artificial" or "analytic" perspective constituted the dominant but not the sole visual model in Renaissance art. Examples of "synthetic" perspective, in which the pictorial surface was conceived as a concave rather than flat mirror, could be found in the work of painters as illustrious as Paolo Uccello and Leonardo da Vinci, while several Renaissance canvases allowed for more than one point of view, that is, did not confine the ideal beholder to a unique position, in a phenomenon called the "robustness" of perspective. Cf. Martin Jay, "Scopic Regimes of Modernity," in *Vision and Visuality*, ed. Hal Foster (Seattle: Bay Press, 1988), 3–23, esp. 10–11.

13. Norman Bryson, *Vision and Painting: The Logic of the Gaze* (New Haven, Conn.: Yale University Press, 1983).

14. For a detailed account of Brunelleschi's two experiments, see Hubert Damisch, *The Origin of Perspective*, trans. John Goodman (Cambridge, Mass.: MIT Press, 1994).

15. Bryson, "The Gaze in the Expanded Field," in *Vision and Visuality*, 89.

16. Ibid., 90–91.

17. For a detailed account of Brunelleschi's first experiment, see Damisch, *Origin of Perspective*, 120–21.

18. The difference coincides with the distinction that film theory draws between primary and secondary identification.

19. Damisch, *Origin of Perspective*, 120.

20. This seems to contradict or question the very premises of perspective, as indicated in "the Latin word *perspectiva*, from *perspicere*, to see clearly, to examine, to ascertain, to see through"; in Martin Jay, *Downcast Eyes* (Berkeley and Los Angeles: University of California Press, 1993), 53.

21. Damisch, *Origin of Perspective*, 157–58.

22. Ibid., 121.

23. On the Heideggerian use of the word *clearing* in relation to *Blow-up*, see Fredric Jameson, *Signatures of the Visible* (New York: Routledge, 1992).

24. Damisch, *Origin of Perspective*, 146.

25. Ibid., 129.

26. Jacques Lacan, *Seminar XI: The Four Fundamental Concepts of Psychoanalysis*, ed. Jacques-Alain Miller, trans. Alan Sheridan (New York: Norton, 1998). Lacan explicitly writes that the fissure between the eye and the gaze constitutes "the split in which the drive is manifested at the level of the scopic field." Ibid., 73.

27. Ibid., 72.

28. Ibid., 106.

29. Ibid., 75.

30. Ibid., 81.

31. Ibid., 85.

32. Ibid., 84.

33. Ibid., 88.

34. On the difference between the gaze and the glance—the latter being linked to the body of the viewer, duration, and intermittent vision, see Bryson, *Vision and Painting*.

35. Lacan, *Seminar XI*, 92. Damisch also emphasizes this aspect in Lacan's interpretation of perspective.

36. Bryson, "Gaze in the Expanded Field," 89.

37. Bryson, *Vision and Painting*, 96.

38. I am referring here to the *fort-da* game. From a Lacanian viewpoint, it is only with the articulation of *da* (there), that *fort* (gone) acquires its meaning—only in the play of difference, in a movement of anticipation and retroaction, that phonemes become significant. By drawing this comparison, I intend not to reduce cinematic vision to a canonical linguistic model but to introduce the possibility of thinking both language and vision as diacritical. I will return to this issue in Chapter 3, as I discuss Merleau-Ponty's late work.

39. Heath, "Narrative Space," 46.

40. Ibid., 48.

41. For a more detailed discussion of this "enactment," see Angelo Restivo, *The Cinema of Economic Miracles: Visuality and Modernization in the Italian Art Film* (Durham, N.C.: Duke University Press, 2002), 110.

42. Marin, "In Praise of Appearance," in *On Representation*, 247.

43. Marie-Claire Ropars-Wuilleumier, "*Blow-up*, ovvero il negativo del racconto," in Bonitzer, *Michelangelo Antonioni*, 2: 38.

44. Ropars-Wuilleumier makes this point in reference to Jorge Luis Borges's "Death and the Compass," a short story to which I shall return in the last chapter.

45. Svetlana Alpers, *The Art of Describing: Dutch Art in the Seventeenth Century* (Chicago: University of Chicago Press, 1983), 37.

46. For this interpretation, I am directly indebted to Pascal Bonitzer's essay on *The Adventure*, "Il concetto di scomparsa," in *Michelangelo Antonioni*. In *Blow-up*, the figure of the "stain" is introduced early on, through the abstract painting, and will return at the very end, when Thomas, shot from a very high angle while standing on the green grass, is transformed into a stain and then made to disappear.

47. Marin, "Depositing Time in Painted Representations," in *On Representation*, 289.

48. See also Ropars-Wuilleumier, *"Blow-up,"* 40.

49. Bryson, *Vision and Painting*, 106.

50. See also Lacan, *Seminar XI*, 96: "That which is gaze is always a play of light and opacity."

51. John Locke, *An Essay Concerning Human Understanding* (Oxford: Clarendon, 1975).

52. Homay King explores the resonance of these words in her beautiful essay " 'All the Shapes We Make': *The Passenger*'s Flight from Formal Stagnation" (contribution to a dossier on film and psychoanalysis), *Qui Parle* 11, no. 2 (Fall–Winter 1999): 115–25.

53. On the visual blockage of the vanishing point in the last shots of *The Passenger* and *The Adventure*, see Kimball Lockhart, "Blockage and Passage in *The Passenger*," *Diacritics* (Spring 1985): 74–84.

54. In *Blow-up* too we find this correspondence between diegesis and enunciation. At the entrance of the park, Thomas's path intersects that of an attendant in uniform, while at the exit it crosses that of a woman and her child.

55. See Fernando Trebbi, *Il testo e lo sguardo* (The Text and the Gaze) (Bologna: Patron, 1976).

56. Damisch, *Origin of Perspective*, 121.

57. Mikkel Borch-Jacobsen, *Lacan: The Absolute Master*, trans. Douglas Brick (Stanford, Calif.: Stanford University Press, 1991), 230.

58. See Lacan, *Seminar XI*, 105: "The *objet a* in the field of the visible is the gaze."

Chapter 2: Desiring Death

1. Quoted in Jacques Lacan, *Seminar XI: The Four Fundamental Concepts of Psychoanalysis*, ed. Jacques-Alain Miller, trans. Alan Sheridan (New York: Norton, 1998), 177.

2. As if I could only begin by repeating, the first part of my reading meticulously draws on Bersani's analysis, almost miming its movement. See Leo Bersani, *The Freudian Body: Psychoanalysis and Art* (New York: Columbia University Press, 1986), 69–77.

3. Ibid., 68.

4. Ibid., 70.

5. Ibid., 78.

6. Against all normalizations of Freud's argument, Jacques Derrida writes that "Freud, no matter what has been said in order vehemently to affirm or contest it, *never*

concludes on this point" (italics in original), the *fort/da* game, the relation between the pleasure principle and the death drive. See *The Post Card: From Socrates to Freud and Beyond*, trans. Alan Bass (Chicago: University of Chicago Press, 1987), 303.

7. Regarding the *fort/da* game, Bersani would instead write that "mastery is simultaneous with self-punishment; a fantasy of omnipotence and autonomy (the child both controls his mother's movements and doesn't need her) is inseparable from a repetition of pain," the pain of separation. He would then add that "an argument *is* being made, but instead of moving 'beyond the pleasure principle,' we are being given a redefinition or an extension of that principle." Bersani, *Freudian Body*, 59.

8. The pleasure principle is here conceived according to a model of discharge. The binding of excitation coinciding with the repetition compulsion occurs independently of but not in opposition to the pleasure principle—indeed, it occurs on its behalf. See Sigmund Freud, *Beyond the Pleasure Principle*, trans. James Strachey (New York: Liveright, 1970).

9. For a reconceptualization of the pleasure principle according to a model of excitation, see Bersani, *Freudian Body*; and Kaja Silverman, *World Spectators* (Stanford, Calif.: Stanford University Press, 2000).

10. See Jean Laplanche, *Life and Death in Psychoanalysis*, trans. Jeffrey Mehlman (Baltimore: Johns Hopkins University Press, 1976).

11. In her introduction to the Italian edition of the screenplay, the director explicitly adopts the term "crime scene" when speaking of the victim's return to the concentration camp. See Liliana Cavani, *Il portiere di notte* (The Night Porter) (Turin: Einaudi, 1974), vii.

12. Lacan, *Seminar XI*, 178.

13. Ibid., 195; italics in original.

14. Kaja Silverman, "Masochism and Subjectivity," *Framework* 12 (1980): 5.

15. See Primo Levi, *The Drowned and the Saved*, trans. Raymond Rosenthal (New York: Random House, 1989).

16. Bersani, *Freudian Body*, 110.

17. Film theorists distinguish between "primary" and "secondary" identification—identification with the apparatus versus identification with the fictional characters. See, for instance, Christian Metz, *The Imaginary Signifier: Psychoanalysis and the Cinema*, trans. Celia Britton, Annwyl Williams, Ben Brewster, and Alfred Guzzetti (Bloomington: Indiana University Press, 1982).

18. Stephen Heath, "Narrative Space," in *Questions of Cinema* (Bloomington: Indiana University Press, 1981), 19–75.

19. See Anne Friedberg, "A Denial of Difference: Theories of Cinematic Identification," in *Psychoanalysis and Cinema*, ed. E. Ann Kaplan (New York: Routledge, 1990), 36–45; and Mary Ann Doane, "Misrecognition and Identity," *Cine-Tracts* 3, no. 3 (1980): 25–32.

20. Kaja Silverman, *The Threshold of the Visible World* (New York: Routledge, 1996).

21. The concept of suture has been pivotal in understanding the relation between cinematic signification and the viewing subject. Theoreticians of suture claim that classical cinema employs the cut, which at once divides and links shots, to conceal the operations of the enunciation and promote secondary identification. Thus lured into the film's fictional world, the spectator experiences, at least intermittently, a sense of coherence and plenitude. Regarding the multifaceted theory of suture, see Daniel Dayan, "The Tutor Code of Classical Cinema," in *Movies and Methods: An Anthology*, ed. Bill Nichols (Berkeley and Los Angeles: University of California Press, 1976), 438–51; Stephen Heath, "Notes on Suture," *Screen* 18, no. 4 (1977–78): 48–76; Jacques-Alain Miller, "Suture (Elements of the Logic of the Signifier)," *Screen* 18, no. 4 (1977–78): 29–34; Jean-Pierre Oudart, "Cinema and Suture," *Screen* 18, no. 4 (1977–78): 35–47. All these articles are discussed in Kaja Silverman, *The Subject of Semiotics* (New York: Oxford University Press, 1983). About *The Night Porter*'s repeated foregrounding of the "cut," at the level of both diegesis and enunciation, see Kaja Silverman, "Masochism and Subjectivity."

22. Freud's notion of identification as incorporation is opposed to Wallon's theorizing of identification according to an excorporative logic. The terms *idiopathic* and *heteropathic* are from Max Scheler, *The Nature of Sympathy*, trans. Peter Heath (1923; reprint, New York: Archon, 1970).

23. See Silverman's chapter on "the bodily ego" in *The Threshold of the Visible World*, which begins by quoting Freud's famous sentence, "the ego is first and foremost a bodily ego," and goes on exploring theorists such as Lacan, Wallon, and Fanon.

24. Béla Balázs, *Theory of the Film: Character and Growth of a New Art*, trans. Edith Bone (New York: Dover, 1970), 48.

25. Balázs enumerates cinema's specific devices in the chapter entitled "A New Form-Language."

26. Silverman reads this last statement as a clear though marginal return to incorporative identification. I believe we could also understand the identification here described as internal to the abduction that has already taken place. If, at the very end, the viewer's own parameters of embodiment seem to prevail again, we might imagine that the look she is now lending to the characters differs from the one that initiated her to the cinematic spectacle, having been transformed by the spectacle itself.

27. The story is drawn from Schopenhauer and quoted by Scheler, in *The Nature of Sympathy*.

28. On the opposition between the bodily ego as a bound/binding form and the death drive as unbinding force, see Laplanche, *Life and Death in Psychoanalysis*, 126:

> Opposite the ego, a binding, vital form, the *death drive* is the last theoretical instance serving to designate a logos that would necessarily be mute, were it to be reduced to its extreme

state . . . the conflict between ego and drive, between defense and "wish fantasy," is neither the sole nor the ultimate form of the opposition between *binding* and *unbinding*. At the unconscious level, within the fantasy—at least if it is considered as something other than "pure" free energy—there must be indeed another more fundamental polarity: life drive and death drive, interdiction and desire.

29. I here refer to masochism as inherently sexual and governed by exciting pain. See Bersani, *Freudian Body*, 62: "in *Beyond the Pleasure Principle* Freud violently manipulates the notion of repetition in order to propose in the death instinct a nonsexual masochism, *a masochism from which exciting pain has been wholly evacuated*" (italics in original).

30. Lacan, *Seminar XI*, 205.

31. See Bersani, *Freudian Body*, 46: "Masochism is both relieved and fulfilled by death, and to stop the play of representations perhaps condemns fantasy to the climactic and suicidal pleasure of mere self-annulment."

32. Samuel Weber argues that the death drive constitutes "just another form of the narcissistic language of the ego," and gives voice to "the need for another form of repetition, to counterbalance that of the death drive (as repetition of the same)." See *The Legend of Freud* (Minneapolis: University of Minnesota Press, 1982), 188.

33. Lacan is explicit in this regard:

Oblivium is that which effaces—effaces what? The signifier as such. Here we find again the basic structure that makes it possible, in an operatory way, for something to take on the function of barring, striking out another thing. This is a more primordial level, structurally speaking, than repression . . . this operatory element of effacement is what Freud designates, from the outset, in the function of the censor. (Lacan, *Seminar XI*, 27)

34. Shoshana Felman and Dori Laub, *Testimony: Crisis of Witnessing in Literature, Psychoanalysis, and History* (New York: Routledge, 1992), 204–5.

35. Quoted in ibid., 204.

36. The expression is used by Walter Benjamin to criticize conventional historiography. See "Theses on the Philosophy of History," in *Illuminations*, ed. Hannah Arendt, trans. Harry Zohn (New York: Schocken, 1968), 255.

37. The reference, explicitly acknowledged by the authors, is to Walter Benjamin, "The Task of the Translator," in *Illuminations*, 69–82.

38. Felman and Laub, *Testimony*, 15; italics in original.

39. Carlo Ginzburg, "Clues: Morelli, Freud, and Sherlock Holmes," in *The Sign of the Three: Dupin, Holmes, Peirce*, ed. Umberto Eco and Thomas A. Sebeok (Bloomington: Indiana University Press, 1983), 81.

40. *The Standard Edition of the Complete Psychological Works of Sigmund Freud*, ed. James Strachey (London: Hogarth, 1953–74), 12: 222.

41. In "A Philosophical View of the Detective Novel," Bloch reminds us of the historical accord between trial and investigation. It is with the shift (in the second half

of the eighteenth century) from the trial by confession to the trial by evidence that the meticulous gathering of clues becomes necessary.

42. See Slavoj Žižek, "Two Ways to Avoid the Real of Desire," in *Looking Awry: An Introduction to Jacques Lacan Through Popular Culture* (Cambridge, Mass.: MIT Press, 1991), 431–39. Unlike the hard-boiled detective, the classical detective maintains an "eccentric position" with respect to the transactions taking place among the suspects. His exteriority is at once enabled and confirmed by the financial reward, the payment he demands.

43. Ibid., 49.

44. Benjamin, "Theses on the Philosophy of History," 263.

45. In "Notes on Afterwardsness," Laplanche refers to what he calls "Freud's consistent rejection of the reversibility of temporal direction." He writes: "In the choice between a deterministic conception that proceeds from the past to the future and a retrospective or hermeneutic conception that proceeds from the future to the past, Freud always chooses the former." Jean Laplanche, "Notes on Afterwardsness," in *Jean Laplanche: Seduction, Translation and the Drives*, ed. John Fletcher and Martin Stanton, trans. Martin Stanton (London: ICA, 1992), 219.

46. Gavin Stevens to Temple Drake Stevens, in William Faulkner, *Requiem for a Nun*, act 1, scene 3 (New York: Vintage, 1975). See also Jean-Luc Godard's videographic experiment *Histoire(s) du cinéma*: "Le Passé n'est jamais mort: Il n'est meme pas passé" (Paris: Gallimard-Gaumont, 1998).

47. Giorgio Agamben, *Remnants of Auschwitz: The Witness and the Archive*, trans. Daniel Heller-Roazen (New York: Zone, 1999), 17.

48. While its etymology is uncertain, in the jargon of the camp the term *Muselmann* or "Muslim" was used to refer to the prisoner who had undergone a process of physical and psychic decay so extreme that she could no longer be considered a "living being." Of these prisoners, the anonymous and countless mass that constituted the majority of the camp's population, Levi writes: "One hesitates to call them living: one hesitates to call their death death, in the face of which they have no fear, as they are too tired to understand." Primo Levi, *Survival in Auschwitz and the Reawakening: Two Memoirs*, trans. Stuart Woolf (New York: Summit, 1986), 90. Agamben reports that these prisoners have also been defined as "mummy-men," "walking corpses," "living dead." Agamben, *Remnants of Auschwitz*, 54.

49. Levi, *Survival in Auschwitz*, 83.

50. Agamben, *Remnants of Auschwitz*, 53–54.

51. Levi, *Survival in Auschwitz*, 84

52. Agamben, *Remnants of Auschwitz*, 150.

53. It is known from witnesses that the SS forbade the living prisoners to refer to the dead as "corpses" or "cadavers." They had to be called *Figuren*, that is, figures, puppets, dolls, or *Schmattes*, which means rags.

Chapter 3: Seeing Time

1. Maurice Merleau-Ponty, *The Visible and the Invisible*, ed. Claude Lefort, trans. Alphonso Lingis (Evanston, Ill.: Northwestern University Press, 1993), 123.

2. Maurice Merleau-Ponty, "Cézanne's Doubt," in *The Merleau-Ponty Aesthetics Reader: Philosophy and Painting*, ed. Galen A. Johnson, trans. Michael Smith (Evanston, Ill.: Northwestern University Press, 1993), 59.

3. Cézanne himself termed such a painting procedure "modulation."

4. Alberto Giacometti, quoted in Merleau-Ponty, "Eye and Mind," in *Merleau-Ponty Aesthetics Reader*, 140.

5. Merleau-Ponty, "Cézanne's Doubt," 64.

6. Ibid., 65.

7. Merleau-Ponty, "Eye and Mind," 135.

8. Ibid., 124. Later in the chapter, I will clarify the peculiar use of the term *narcissism*.

9. Merleau-Ponty explicitly states that "the world is made of the very stuff of the body." Ibid., 125. To the notion of "flesh," which the term "stuff" anticipates, I will devote the last section of this chapter.

10. On this interpenetration, Merleau-Ponty writes: "The painter's vision is not a view upon the *outside*, a merely 'physical-optical' relation with the world. The world no longer stands before him through representation; rather it is the painter to whom the things of the world give birth by a sort of concentration or coming-to-itself of the visible." Merleau-Ponty, "Eye and Mind," 141.

11. Merleau-Ponty, "Cézanne's Doubt," 60.

12. In "Eye and Mind," 130, Merleau-Ponty writes of Descartes' *Dioptrics* that it is "the breviary of a thought that wants no longer to abide in the visible and so decides to reconstruct it according to a model-in-thought."

13. Ernst Bloch, "A Philosophical View of the Detective Novel," *The Utopian Function of Art and Literature*, trans. Jack Zipes and Frank Mecklenburg (Cambridge, Mass.: MIT Press, 1988), 245–64.

14. Slavoj Žižek, "Two Ways to Avoid the Real of Desire," in *Looking Awry: An Introduction to Jacques Lacan Through Popular Culture* (Cambridge, Mass.: MIT Press, 1991), 53.

15. In this regard, Žižek refers to Lacan and his claim that "in every structure there is a lure, a place-holder of the lack, comprised by what is perceived, but at the same time the weakest link in a given series, the point which vacillates." Ibid., 53. I am also reminded of Freud's allusion to the Nibelungen saga:

> If the first account given me by a patient of a dream is too hard to follow I ask him to repeat it. In doing so he rarely uses the same words. But the parts of the dream which he describes in different terms are by that fact revealed to me as the weak spot in the dream's disguise: they serve my purpose just as Hagen was served by the embroidered mark on Siegfried's cloak. (Sigmund Freud, *The Interpretation of Dreams*, trans. James Strachey [New York: Avon, 1965], 553)

Freud speaks here of the small cross which Kriemhild was persuaded to embroider on Siegfried's cloak to mark the only spot where he could be wounded.

16. The screenplay describes the child seeing the world in "bits and pieces"—arms grabbing him, legs running around in circle.

17. Merleau-Ponty, "Eye and Mind," 127.

18. Merleau-Ponty, "Cézanne's Doubt," 65.

19. However, it would be a mistake to conceive "light as an action by contact—not unlike the action of things upon the blind's man cane," thus modeling vision after the sense of touch, according to the Cartesian model of vision. Instead, light is "action at a distance." See Merleau-Ponty, "Eye and Mind," 131, 138.

20. Merleau-Ponty, *The Visible and the Invisible*, 134.

21. Merleau-Ponty, "Eye and Mind," 129.

22. Pier Paolo Pasolini, "The Cinema of Poetry," in *Heretical Empiricism*, ed. Louise K. Barnett, trans. Ben Lawton and Louise K. Barnett (Bloomington: Indiana University Press), 184.

23. Ibid., 179; italics in original.

24. Judith Butler theorizes the temporality of the curse with respect to Antigone in *Antigone's Claim: Kinship Between Life and Death* (New York: Columbia University Press, 2000). Here, in the place of Antigone, we find Angelo, the messenger (played by Pasolini's beloved Ninetto Davoli), perhaps a disturbance in the order of time and kinship imposed by the Oedipus complex.

25. Naomi Greene, *Pier Paolo Pasolini: Cinema as Heresy* (Princeton, N.J.: Princeton University Press, 1990), 152.

26. Ibid., 154.

27. See Massimo Fusillo, *La Grecia secondo Pasolini: Mito e cinema* (Greece According to Pasolini: Myth and Cinema) (Florence: Nuova Italia, 1996).

28. Shoshana Felman, *Jacques Lacan and the Adventures of Insight: Psychoanalysis in Contemporary Culture* (Cambridge, Mass.: Harvard University Press), 147.

29. Jacques Lacan, *The Seminar of Jacques Lacan, Book II: The Ego in Freud's Theory and in the Technique of Psychoanalysis, 1954–1955*, ed. Jacques-Alain Miller, trans. John Forrester (New York: Norton, 1991), 209.

30. Ibid., 214.

31. See Felman, *Jacques Lacan and the Adventures of Insight*, 134: "Oedipus *is born*, through the assumption of his death (of his radical self-expropriation), *into the life of his history*" (italics in original). In the next chapter, I will further address the significance of such assumption through Lacan's notion of full speech.

32. Gilles Deleuze, *Cinema 1: The Movement-Image*, trans. Hugh Tomlinson and Barbara Habberjam (Minneapolis: University of Minnesota Press, 1986), 74.

33. For Merleau-Ponty, language and vision can be folded upon each other and constitute a chiasm.

34. Merleau-Ponty, *The Visible and the Invisible*, 117.

35. Ibid., 11.

36. Béla Balázs, *Theory of the Film: Character and Growth of a New Art*, trans. Edith Bone (New York: Dover, 1970), 40.

37. Ibid., 41.

38. Ibid., 62.

39. Ibid., 58.

40. Ibid., 92.

41. Ibid., 96.

42. Ibid., 56.

43. Ibid., 96.

44. Ibid., 92.

45. Merleau-Ponty, "The Film and the New Psychology," in *Sense and Non-Sense*, trans. Hubert L. Dreyfus and Patricia Allen Dreyfus (Evanston, Ill.: Northwestern University Press, 1964), 48–59.

46. Merleau-Ponty, *The Visible and the Invisible*, 140.

47. Ibid., 147.

48. Ibid., 136.

49. However, Merleau-Ponty warns us, it would be reductive to consider the example of the hands touching each other as a metaphor adopted to elucidate what happens elsewhere, in a separate domain. Vision and touch, the visible and the tangible must no longer be thought in isolation. He writes:

> We must habituate ourselves to think that every visible is cut out in the tangible, every tactile being in some manner promised to visibility, and that there is encroachment, infringement, not only between the touched and the touching, but also between the tangible and the visible, which is encrusted in it, as, conversely, the tangible itself is not a nothingness of visibility, is not without visual existence. Since the same body sees and touches, visible and tangible belong to the same world. (Merleau-Ponty, *The Visible and the Invisible*, 134)

50. Ibid., 255. See also "Eye and Mind," 129:

> The mirror image anticipates, within things, the labor of vision. Like all other technical objects . . . the mirror has sprung up along the open circuit *between* the seeing and the visible body. Every technique is a "technique of the body," illustrating and amplifying the metaphysical structure of our flesh. The mirror emerges because I am a visible see-er, because there is a reflexivity of the sensible; the mirror translates and reproduces that reflexivity. In it, my externality becomes complete. Everything that is most secret about me passes into that face, that flat, closed being of which I was already dimly aware, from having seen my reflection mirrored in water.

51. Merleau-Ponty, *The Visible and the Invisible*, 139.

52. In "Merleau-Ponty and the Touch of Malebranche," Judith Butler writes of this vision that defies the very distinction between activity and passivity: "Something sees

through me as I see. I see with a seeing that is not mine alone. I see, and as I see, the I that I am is put at risk, discovers its derivation from what is permanently enigmatic to itself." *The Cambridge Companion to Merleau-Ponty*, ed. Taylor Carman and Mark B. Hansen (Cambridge, U.K.: Cambridge University Press, 2005), 202.

53. Merleau-Ponty, *The Visible and the Invisible*, 142.

54. See ibid., 201: "the *self* of perception as 'nobody,' in the sense of Ulysses, as the anonymous one buried in the world."

55. On time and the flesh, see Glen A. Mazis, "Merleau-Ponty and the 'Backward Flow' of Time: The Reversibility of Temporality and the Temporality of Reversibility," in *Merleau-Ponty, Hermeneutics, and Postmodernism*, ed. Thomas W. Busch and Shaun Gallagher (Albany: State University of New York Press, 1992), 53–68; and Dorothea Olkowski, "Merleau-Ponty's Freudianism: From the Body of Consciousness to the Body of the Flesh," in *Review of Existential Psychology and Psychiatry* 18, nos. 1–3 (1982–83): 97–116.

56. Merleau-Ponty, *The Visible and the Invisible*, 268.

57. Ibid., 267.

58. Ibid., 184.

59. Ibid., 147.

60. Ibid., 114.

61. Ibid., 267 and 195.

62. Ibid., 240.

63. Freud, "Remembering, Repeating, and Working-Through," in *The Standard Edition of the Complete Psychological Works of Sigmund Freud*, ed. James Strachey (London: Hogarth, 1953–74), 12: 82.

64. Merleau-Ponty, *The Visible and the Invisible*, 270.

65. In the form of a note, he writes: "Understand that 'to be conscious' = to have a figure on a ground." Ibid., 197. See James Phillips, "From the Unseen to the Invisible: Merleau-Ponty's Sorbonne Lectures as Preparation for His Later Thought," in *Merleau-Ponty, Interiority and Exteriority, Psychic Life and the World*, ed. Dorothea Olkowski and James Morley (Albany: State University of New York Press, 1999), 69–88.

66. Merleau-Ponty, *The Visible and the Invisible*, 215.

67. Ibid., 180.

68. Ibid., 263.

69. Ibid., 132.

70. Merleau-Ponty states that "vision, thought are structured like a language, are *articulation*," that "perception [is] a diacritical, relative, oppositional system." Ibid., 126, 213.

71. Ibid., 240.

72. Ibid., 194.

Chapter 4: Twilight

1. Jacques Lacan, *Seminar XI: The Four Fundamental Concepts of Psychoanalysis*, ed. Jacques-Alain Miller, trans. Alan Sheridan (New York: Norton, 1998), 93.

2. John Ruskin, *Fors Clavigera* (1872), in *Works of John Ruskin*, ed. E. T. Cook and Alexander Wedderburn (London: Allen, 1907), vol. 27.

3. Paolo Santarcangeli, *Il libro dei labirinti: Storia di un mito e di un simbolo* (The Book of Labyrinths: History of a Myth and of a Symbol), introduced by Umberto Eco (Milan: Frassinelli, 1984).

4. Ibid., 3 (my translation).

5. J. Hillis Miller, *Ariadne's Thread: Story Lines* (New Haven, Conn.: Yale University Press, 1992), 17.

6. Italo Calvino, *Six Memos for the Next Millennium*, trans. Patrick Creagh (Cambridge, Mass.: Harvard University Press, 1988).

7. I am indebted to Miller for this interpretation of the story's ending.

8. Jorge Luis Borges, *Collected Fictions*, trans. Andrew Hurley (New York: Penguin, 1998), 127.

9. Calvino, *Six Memos*, 129. Among the passages of Borges that inspired Calvino's reading of him: "Then I reflected that all things happen to *oneself*, and happen precisely, precisely *now*. Century follows century, yet events occur only *in the present*; countless men in the air, on the land and sea, yet everything that truly happens, happens *to me*." *"He who is to perform a horrendous act should imagine to himself that it is already done, should impose upon himself a future as irrevocable as the past."* "The *Garden of Forking Paths* is a huge riddle, or parable, whose subject is time." "That fabric of times that approach one another, fork, are snipped off, or are simply unknown for centuries, contains *all* possibilities." Borges, *Collected Fictions*, 120, 121, 126, 127; italics in original.

10. Ibid., 144.

11. Hereafter, to reduce but not eliminate the film's ambiguity, I will refer to the son as Athos and to the father as Athos Magnani.

12. Jacques Lacan, "The Function and Field of Speech and Language in Psychoanalysis," in *Écrits: A Selection*, trans. Alan Sheridan (New York: Norton, 1977), 69.

13. Angela Dalle Vacche, *The Body in the Mirror: Shapes of History in Italian Cinema* (Princeton, N.J.: Princeton University Press, 1992), 229.

14. Bernardo Bertolucci, quoted in Enzo Ungari, *Scene madri* (Mother Scenes) (Milan: Ubulibri, 1982), 117.

15. For a brief "history of light" in the metaphysical tradition, see Hans Blumenberg, "Light as a Metaphor for Truth: At the Preliminary Stage of Philosophical Concept Formation," in *Modernity and the Hegemony of Vision*, ed. David Michael Levin (Berkeley and Los Angeles: University of California Press, 1993), 30–62.

16. Lacan, "The Function and Field," 65.

17. Ibid., 69.

18. Ibid., 42.

19. Ibid., 86.

20. Ibid.

21. Ibid., 103.

22. "What is waiting to be revealed is being. . . . Depending on the way one envisions it, this hole in the real is called being or nothingness. This being and this nothingness are essentially linked to the phenomenon of speech." Jacques Lacan, *The Seminar of Jacques Lacan, Book I: Freud's Papers on Technique, 1953–1954*, ed. Jacques-Alain Miller, trans. John Forrester (New York: Norton, 1991), 270–71.

23. Lacan, quoted in Mikkel Borch-Jacobsen, *Lacan: The Absolute Master*, trans. Douglas Birk (Stanford, Calif.: Stanford University Press), 137.

24. Borch-Jacobsen, *Lacan*, 111.

25. Lacan, *Seminar I*, 109.

26. Kaja Silverman, *World Spectators* (Stanford, Calif.: Stanford University Press, 2000), 71.

27. In Chapter 1, I provide a detailed reading of Lacan's seminar on the gaze.

28. Lacan, *Seminar XI*, 95.

29. On the ego, Lacan writes: "This ego, whose strength our theorists now define by its capacity to bear frustration, is frustration in its essence. Not frustration of a desire of the subject, but frustration by an object in which his desire is alienated and which the more it is elaborated, the more profound the alienation from his *jouissance* becomes for the subject." Lacan, *Écrits*, 42.

30. Lacan, *Seminar XI*, 82.

31. Maurice Merleau-Ponty, *The Visible and the Invisible*, ed. Claude Lefort, trans. Alphonso Lingis (Evanston, Ill.: Northwestern University Press, 1993), 201

32. Ibid., 194.

33. Lacan, *Seminar XI*, 75.

34. In *World Spectators*, Silverman argues that Freud himself comes to contradict his own famous claim that all dreams are "completely egoistic: the beloved ego appears in all of them, even though it might be disguised." In chapter 7 of *Interpretation of Dreams*, Silverman points out, the dreamer is compared not to the hero of a story, but to a play writer, whose aim is *showing* someone else rather than *seeing* himself in multiple roles.

35. See Robert Phillip Kolker, *Bernardo Bertolucci* (New York: Oxford University Press, 1985), for an analysis of *Rigoletto*'s story of masquerades and mistaken identities and its relevance to the film.

36. The expression is used by Walter Benjamin in his critique of conventional historiography. See "Theses on the Philosophy of History," in *Illuminations*, ed. Hannah Arendt, trans. Harry Zohn (New York: Schocken, 1968), 255.

37. An emphasis on self-same repetition characterizes the dominant reading of the

film. See, for instance, Angela Dalle Vacche, *The Body in the Mirror: Shapes of History in Italian Cinema* (Princeton, N.J.: Princeton University Press, 1992); and Robert Phillip Kolker, *Bernardo Bertolucci* (New York: Oxford University Press, 1985).

38. Maurice Merleau-Ponty, *Phenomenology of Perception*, trans. Colin Smith (London: Routledge and Kegan Paul, 1962), 242.

39. Miller, *Ariadne's Thread*, 18.

40. From the point of view of the past on the rooftop, the present of the square becomes the future that will have been—from the point of view of the present in the square, the past on the rooftop becomes the past that will have been.

41. This is the statue on which the words "hero vilely murdered by fascist bullets" are inscribed. It first appears after Athos's arrival and then returns several times throughout the film.

42. Lacan, *Écrits*, 104.

43. Merleau-Ponty, *The Visible and the Invisible*, 146.

Index